#ANOTE2SELF

—

Meditation Journal

by

Alex Elle

#Anote2self Meditation Journal

By Alex Elle

All Rights Reserved.

Additional content by:

Carolyn Nash, Jack Stewart, Nicole Wong, Harrison Gorman,
Destiny Janae, Dru Arroyo, Katherine Pelfrey.

Art Direction & Design by Laura Pol

Concept by Alex Elle

—

Dear Self,

Write your heart out.

Love,
Self

"COMMIT YOURSELF TO LOVE, EVOLUTION & SELF PRESERVATION"

DATE: /   /   ●   TIME   :

WHAT DOES IT MEAN TO LOVE YOURSELF?

DEAR SELF,

MY INTENTIONS FOR TODAY ARE

1.
2.
3.

I AM THANKFUL FOR

I WILL ACCOMPLISH THESE THINGS TODAY

1.
2.
3.

I AM GOING TO ENJOY

1.
2.
3.

I NEED TO WORK ON

1.
2.

min - *1   2   3   4   5   6   7   8   9   10   11   12   13   14   15*

#anote2self

DATE: /   /   ●   TIME   :

WHAT ARE SOME BARRIERS THAT GET IN THE WAY OF SELF-LOVE?

DEAR SELF,

MY INTENTIONS FOR TODAY ARE

1.
2.
3.

I AM THANKFUL FOR

I WILL ACCOMPLISH THESE THINGS TODAY

1.
2.
3.

I AM GOING TO ENJOY

1.
2.
3.

I NEED TO WORK ON

1.
2.

min - 1   2   3   4   5   6   7   8   9   10   11   12   13   14   15

#anote2self

DATE: /   /   ●   TIME   :

WHAT BENEFITS COME FROM LOVING YOURSELF?

DEAR SELF,

MY INTENTIONS FOR TODAY ARE

1.
2.
3.

I AM THANKFUL FOR

I WILL ACCOMPLISH THESE THINGS TODAY

1.
2.
3.

I AM GOING TO ENJOY

1.
2.
3.

I NEED TO WORK ON

1.
2.

min - 1   2   3   4   5   6   7   8   9   10   11   12   13   14   15

#anote2self

DATE: /   /   ● 　　　　　　TIME   :

DESCRIBE YOURSELF IN FIVE WORDS.

_____
_____
_____
_____

DEAR SELF,

_____
_____
_____
_____

MY INTENTIONS FOR TODAY ARE

1. _____
2. _____
3. _____

I AM THANKFUL FOR

_____

I WILL ACCOMPLISH THESE THINGS TODAY

1. _____
2. _____
3. _____

I AM GOING TO ENJOY

1. _____
2. _____
3. _____

I NEED TO WORK ON

1. _____
2. _____

min - 1   2   3   4   5   6   7   8   9   10   11   12   13   14   15

#anote2self

DATE: /   /   ◗   TIME   :

WHY DO YOU LOVE YOURSELF?

_____
_____
_____
_____

DEAR SELF,

_____
_____
_____
_____

MY INTENTIONS FOR TODAY ARE

1. _____
2. _____
3. _____

I AM THANKFUL FOR

_____

I WILL ACCOMPLISH THESE THINGS TODAY

1. _____
2. _____
3. _____

I AM GOING TO ENJOY

1. _____
2. _____
3. _____

I NEED TO WORK ON

1. _____
2. _____

min - 1   2   3   4   5   6   7   8   9   10   11   12   13   14   15

#anote2self

DATE: / / TIME :

DESCRIBE THE MOMENT YOU REALIZED YOU LOVED YOURSELF.

DEAR SELF,

MY INTENTIONS FOR TODAY ARE

1.
2.
3.

I AM THANKFUL FOR

I WILL ACCOMPLISH THESE THINGS TODAY

1.
2.
3.

I AM GOING TO ENJOY

1.
2.
3.

I NEED TO WORK ON

1.
2.

min - 1 2 3 4 5 6 7 8 9 10 11 12 13 14 15

#anote2self

DATE: /   /   ◑   TIME   :

WHAT INSPIRES YOU TO BE WHO YOU ARE?

DEAR SELF,

MY INTENTIONS FOR TODAY ARE

1.
2.
3.

I AM THANKFUL FOR

I WILL ACCOMPLISH THESE THINGS TODAY

1.
2.
3.

I AM GOING TO ENJOY

1.
2.
3.

I NEED TO WORK ON

1.
2.

min - 1   2   3   4   5   6   7   8   9   10   11   12   13   14   15

#anote2self

DATE: /   /   ●   TIME   :

DOES DECADENCE PLAY A ROLE IN SELF-LOVE?

_____
_____
_____
_____

DEAR SELF,

_____
_____
_____
_____

MY INTENTIONS FOR TODAY ARE

1. _____
2. _____
3. _____

I AM THANKFUL FOR

_____

I WILL ACCOMPLISH THESE THINGS TODAY

1. _____
2. _____
3. _____

I AM GOING TO ENJOY

1. _____
2. _____
3. _____

I NEED TO WORK ON

1. _____
2. _____

min - _1   2   3   4   5   6   7   8   9   10   11   12   13   14   15_

#anote2self

DATE: /   /   ◐   TIME   :

HOW DO YOU KNOW YOU HAVE HEALED?

_____
_____
_____
_____

DEAR SELF,

_____
_____
_____
_____

MY INTENTIONS FOR TODAY ARE

1. _____
2. _____
3. _____

I AM THANKFUL FOR

_____

I WILL ACCOMPLISH THESE THINGS TODAY

1. _____
2. _____
3. _____

I AM GOING TO ENJOY

1. _____
2. _____
3. _____

I NEED TO WORK ON

1. _____
2. _____

min - 1   2   3   4   5   6   7   8   9   10   11   12   13   14   15

#anote2self

DATE: /   /   ◐   TIME   :

WHAT CAN BLOCK HEALING? WHAT CAN UNBLOCK HEALING?

DEAR SELF,

MY INTENTIONS FOR TODAY ARE
1.
2.
3.

I AM THANKFUL FOR

I WILL ACCOMPLISH THESE THINGS TODAY
1.
2.
3.

I AM GOING TO ENJOY
1.
2.
3.

I NEED TO WORK ON
1.
2.

min - 1   2   3   4   5   6   7   8   9   10   11   12   13   14   15

#anote2self

DATE: / / ◐ TIME :

HOW MANY MAJOR HEALING PROCESSES HAVE YOU EXPERIENCED?

_____
_____
_____
_____

DEAR SELF,

_____
_____
_____
_____

MY INTENTIONS FOR TODAY ARE

1. _____
2. _____
3. _____

I AM THANKFUL FOR

_____

I WILL ACCOMPLISH THESE THINGS TODAY

1. _____
2. _____
3. _____

I AM GOING TO ENJOY

1. _____
2. _____
3. _____

I NEED TO WORK ON

1. _____
2. _____

min - *1 2 3 4 5 6 7 8 9 10 11 12 13 14 15*

#anote2self

DATE: /   /   ◖   TIME   :

WHAT STEPS DO YOU TAKE TO HEAL?

_____
_____
_____
_____

DEAR SELF,

_____
_____
_____
_____

MY INTENTIONS FOR TODAY ARE

1. _____
2. _____
3. _____

I AM THANKFUL FOR

_____

I WILL ACCOMPLISH THESE THINGS TODAY

1. _____
2. _____
3. _____

I AM GOING TO ENJOY

1. _____
2. _____
3. _____

I NEED TO WORK ON

1. _____
2. _____

min - 1   2   3   4   5   6   7   8   9   10   11   12   13   14   15

#anote2self

DATE: / / ◐ TIME :

IS IT POSSIBLE TO HELP OTHERS HEAL?

_____
_____
_____
_____

DEAR SELF,

_____
_____
_____
_____

MY INTENTIONS FOR TODAY ARE

1. _____
2. _____
3. _____

I AM THANKFUL FOR

_____

I WILL ACCOMPLISH THESE THINGS TODAY

1. _____
2. _____
3. _____

I AM GOING TO ENJOY

1. _____
2. _____
3. _____

I NEED TO WORK ON

1. _____
2. _____

min - 1 2 3 4 5 6 7 8 9 10 11 12 13 14 15

#anote2self

DATE: / /   TIME   :

WHY IS IT DIFFICULT TO HEAL SOMETIMES?

_____
_____
_____
_____

DEAR SELF,

_____
_____
_____
_____

MY INTENTIONS FOR TODAY ARE

1. _____
2. _____
3. _____

I AM THANKFUL FOR

_____

I WILL ACCOMPLISH THESE THINGS TODAY

1. _____
2. _____
3. _____

I AM GOING TO ENJOY

1. _____
2. _____
3. _____

I NEED TO WORK ON

1. _____
2. _____

min - *1   2   3   4   5   6   7   8   9   10   11   12   13   14   15*

#anote2self

DATE: / / TIME :

IS THERE SOMETHING FROM WHICH YOU'VE YET TO HEAL?

DEAR SELF,

MY INTENTIONS FOR TODAY ARE

1.
2.
3.

I AM THANKFUL FOR

I WILL ACCOMPLISH THESE THINGS TODAY

1.
2.
3.

I AM GOING TO ENJOY

1.
2.
3.

I NEED TO WORK ON

1.
2.

min - 1 2 3 4 5 6 7 8 9 10 11 12 13 14 15

#anote2self

DATE: /   /   ◯   TIME   :

IS HEALING VITAL TO ACHIEVING HAPPINESS FOR YOURSELF?

_____
_____
_____
_____

DEAR SELF,

_____
_____
_____
_____

MY INTENTIONS FOR TODAY ARE

1. _____
2. _____
3. _____

I AM THANKFUL FOR

_____

I WILL ACCOMPLISH THESE THINGS TODAY

1. _____
2. _____
3. _____

I AM GOING TO ENJOY

1. _____
2. _____
3. _____

I NEED TO WORK ON

1. _____
2. _____

min - 1   2   3   4   5   6   7   8   9   10   11   12   13   14   15

#anote2self

DATE: /   /   ◑   TIME   :

DO YOU TRUST IN YOUR FAITH RATHER THAN TRUSTING YOURSELF TO
DRIVE THE HEALING PROCESS?

_____
_____
_____

DEAR SELF,

_____
_____
_____
_____

MY INTENTIONS FOR TODAY ARE

1. _____
2. _____
3. _____

I AM THANKFUL FOR

_____

I WILL ACCOMPLISH THESE THINGS TODAY

1. _____
2. _____
3. _____

I AM GOING TO ENJOY

1. _____
2. _____
3. _____

I NEED TO WORK ON

1. _____
2. _____

min - 1   2   3   4   5   6   7   8   9   10   11   12   13   14   15

#anote2self

DATE: /   /   ◐   TIME   :

HOW DID YOUR INTERNAL GROWTH HELP TRANSPORT YOU TO WHERE
YOU ARE TODAY?

DEAR SELF,

MY INTENTIONS FOR TODAY ARE

1.
2.
3.

I AM THANKFUL FOR

I WILL ACCOMPLISH THESE THINGS TODAY

1.
2.
3.

I AM GOING TO ENJOY

1.
2.
3.

I NEED TO WORK ON

1.
2.

min - 1   2   3   4   5   6   7   8   9   10   11   12   13   14   15

#anote2self

DATE: / / ☽ TIME :

WAS THERE A MOMENT WHEN YOU REALIZED IT WAS TIME TO GROW OUT OF YOUR STAGNATION?

DEAR SELF,

MY INTENTIONS FOR TODAY ARE

1.
2.
3.

I AM THANKFUL FOR

I WILL ACCOMPLISH THESE THINGS TODAY

1.
2.
3.

I AM GOING TO ENJOY

1.
2.
3.

I NEED TO WORK ON

1.
2.

min - 1 2 3 4 5 6 7 8 9 10 11 12 13 14 15

#anote2self

DATE: /   /   ◑   TIME   :

WHAT ARE SOME EXTERNAL BARRIERS THAT CAN STUNT YOUR GROWTH?

DEAR SELF,

MY INTENTIONS FOR TODAY ARE

1.
2.
3.

I AM THANKFUL FOR

I WILL ACCOMPLISH THESE THINGS TODAY

1.
2.
3.

I AM GOING TO ENJOY

1.
2.
3.

I NEED TO WORK ON

1.
2.

min - 1   2   3   4   5   6   7   8   9   10   11   12   13   14   15

#anote2self

DATE: /   /   ◑   TIME   :

IN ORDER TO GROW, WHAT ARE SOME INTERNAL THINGS OF WHICH WE
MUST RID OURSELVES?

DEAR SELF,

MY INTENTIONS FOR TODAY ARE

1.
2.
3.

I AM THANKFUL FOR

I WILL ACCOMPLISH THESE THINGS TODAY

1.
2.
3.

I AM GOING TO ENJOY

1.
2.
3.

I NEED TO WORK ON

1.
2.

min - 1   2   3   4   5   6   7   8   9   10   11   12   13   14   15

#anote2self

DATE: / / TIME :

DO YOU PROMOTE GROWTH IN OTHERS?

DEAR SELF,

MY INTENTIONS FOR TODAY ARE
1.
2.
3.

I AM THANKFUL FOR

I WILL ACCOMPLISH THESE THINGS TODAY
1.
2.
3.

I AM GOING TO ENJOY
1.
2.
3.

I NEED TO WORK ON
1.
2.

min - 1 2 3 4 5 6 7 8 9 10 11 12 13 14 15

#anote2self

DATE: / / ◐ TIME :

HOW DO YOU CONQUER FEAR OF GROWING?

_____
_____
_____
_____

DEAR SELF,

_____
_____
_____
_____

MY INTENTIONS FOR TODAY ARE

1. _____
2. _____
3. _____

I AM THANKFUL FOR

_____

I WILL ACCOMPLISH THESE THINGS TODAY

1. _____
2. _____
3. _____

I AM GOING TO ENJOY

1. _____
2. _____
3. _____

I NEED TO WORK ON

1. _____
2. _____

DATE: /   /   ◑   TIME   :

WHAT ARE SOME CHARACTERISTICS THAT DESCRIBE YOU?

DEAR SELF,

MY INTENTIONS FOR TODAY ARE

1.
2.
3.

I AM THANKFUL FOR

I WILL ACCOMPLISH THESE THINGS TODAY

1.
2.
3.

I AM GOING TO ENJOY

1.
2.
3.

I NEED TO WORK ON

1.
2.

min - *1   2   3   4   5   6   7   8   9   10   11   12   13   14   15*

#anote2self

DATE: / / TIME :

WHAT ARE SOME WAYS THAT YOU'VE GROWN?

_____
_____
_____
_____

DEAR SELF,

_____
_____
_____
_____

MY INTENTIONS FOR TODAY ARE

1. _____
2. _____
3. _____

I AM THANKFUL FOR

_____

I WILL ACCOMPLISH THESE THINGS TODAY

1. _____
2. _____
3. _____

I AM GOING TO ENJOY

1. _____
2. _____
3. _____

I NEED TO WORK ON

1. _____
2. _____

min - 1 2 3 4 5 6 7 8 9 10 11 12 13 14 15

#anote2self

DATE: /   /   ◑   TIME   :

WHAT IS YOUR FAVORITE WAY TO SHOW LOVE?

_____
_____
_____
_____

DEAR SELF,

_____
_____
_____
_____

MY INTENTIONS FOR TODAY ARE

1. _____
2. _____
3. _____

I AM THANKFUL FOR

_____

I WILL ACCOMPLISH THESE THINGS TODAY

1. _____
2. _____
3. _____

I AM GOING TO ENJOY

1. _____
2. _____
3. _____

I NEED TO WORK ON

1. _____
2. _____

min - 1   2   3   4   5   6   7   8   9   10   11   12   13   14   15

#anote2self

DATE: / /　　　　　　　●　　　　　　TIME :

HOW CAN SELF-LOVE HELP YOU LOVE OTHERS?

DEAR SELF,

MY INTENTIONS FOR TODAY ARE

1.
2.
3.

I AM THANKFUL FOR

I WILL ACCOMPLISH THESE THINGS TODAY

1.
2.
3.

I AM GOING TO ENJOY

1.
2.
3.

I NEED TO WORK ON

1.
2.

min - *1 2 3 4 5 6 7 8 9 10 11 12 13 14 15*

#anote2self

DATE: /   /   ●   TIME   :

DO YOU FEEL SELFISH FOR PUTTING YOURSELF FIRST?

DEAR SELF,

MY INTENTIONS FOR TODAY ARE

1.
2.
3.

I AM THANKFUL FOR

I WILL ACCOMPLISH THESE THINGS TODAY

1.
2.
3.

I AM GOING TO ENJOY

1.
2.
3.

I NEED TO WORK ON

1.
2.

min - 1   2   3   4   5   6   7   8   9   10   11   12   13   14   15

#anote2self

"YOUR JOURNEY ISN'T ALWAYS GOING TO EMBODY CLEAR SKIES
AND SUNSHINE. KNOW THAT YOUR STORM CLOUDS AND POURING RAIN
IS WORTH IT"

DATE: / /   ●   TIME   :

WHAT MOMENTS IN YOUR LIFE INSPIRE YOU TO MEDITATE?

DEAR SELF,

MY INTENTIONS FOR TODAY ARE

1.
2.
3.

I AM THANKFUL FOR

I WILL ACCOMPLISH THESE THINGS TODAY

1.
2.
3.

I AM GOING TO ENJOY

1.
2.
3.

I NEED TO WORK ON

1.
2.

min - *1   2   3   4   5   6   7   8   9   10   11   12   13   14   15*

#anote2self

DATE: / /　　　　　●　　　　　TIME :

IS MEDITATION JUST AN OUTLET FOR RELEASING NEGATIVE ENERGY?

DEAR SELF,

MY INTENTIONS FOR TODAY ARE

1.
2.
3.

I AM THANKFUL FOR

I WILL ACCOMPLISH THESE THINGS TODAY

1.
2.
3.

I AM GOING TO ENJOY

1.
2.
3.

I NEED TO WORK ON

1.
2.

min - 1 2 3 4 5 6 7 8 9 10 11 12 13 14 15

#anote2self

DATE: / /   ●   TIME :

HOW DOES MEDITATION INSPIRE YOU TO SELF-PRESERVE?

DEAR SELF,

MY INTENTIONS FOR TODAY ARE

1.
2.
3.

I AM THANKFUL FOR

I WILL ACCOMPLISH THESE THINGS TODAY

1.
2.
3.

I AM GOING TO ENJOY

1.
2.
3.

I NEED TO WORK ON

1.
2.

min - 1 2 3 4 5 6 7 8 9 10 11 12 13 14 15

#anote2self

DATE: /   /   ●   TIME   :

HOW CAN MEDITATION LEAD TO HAPPINESS?

DEAR SELF,

MY INTENTIONS FOR TODAY ARE

1.
2.
3.

I AM THANKFUL FOR

I WILL ACCOMPLISH THESE THINGS TODAY

1.
2.
3.

I AM GOING TO ENJOY

1.
2.
3.

I NEED TO WORK ON

1.
2.

min - 1   2   3   4   5   6   7   8   9   10   11   12   13   14   15

#anote2self

DATE: / / TIME :

HOW CAN MEDITATION ASSIST IN SELF-SOOTHING?

DEAR SELF,

MY INTENTIONS FOR TODAY ARE
1.
2.
3.

I AM THANKFUL FOR

I WILL ACCOMPLISH THESE THINGS TODAY
1.
2.
3.

I AM GOING TO ENJOY
1.
2.
3.

I NEED TO WORK ON
1.
2.

min - *1 2 3 4 5 6 7 8 9 10 11 12 13 14 15*

#anote2self

DATE: / /　　　　　　🌗　　　　　　　TIME ：

WHAT DOES MEDITATION MEAN TO YOU?

DEAR SELF,

MY INTENTIONS FOR TODAY ARE

1.
2.
3.

I AM THANKFUL FOR

I WILL ACCOMPLISH THESE THINGS TODAY

1.
2.
3.

I AM GOING TO ENJOY

1.
2.
3.

I NEED TO WORK ON

1.
2.

min - *1 2 3 4 5 6 7 8 9 10 11 12 13 14 15*

#anote2self

DATE: /   /   ◐   TIME   :

WHAT RELATIONSHIP DO ART AND MEDITATION SHARE?

_____
_____
_____
_____

DEAR SELF,

_____
_____
_____
_____

MY INTENTIONS FOR TODAY ARE

1. _____
2. _____
3. _____

I AM THANKFUL FOR

_____

I WILL ACCOMPLISH THESE THINGS TODAY

1. _____
2. _____
3. _____

I AM GOING TO ENJOY

1. _____
2. _____
3. _____

I NEED TO WORK ON

1. _____
2. _____

min - 1   2   3   4   5   6   7   8   9   10   11   12   13   14   15

#anote2self

DATE: / /　　　　　　◑　　　　　　TIME :

ARE YOU HAPPY? WHY OR WHY NOT?

DEAR SELF,

MY INTENTIONS FOR TODAY ARE

1.
2.
3.

I AM THANKFUL FOR

I WILL ACCOMPLISH THESE THINGS TODAY

1.
2.
3.

I AM GOING TO ENJOY

1.
2.
3.

I NEED TO WORK ON

1.
2.

min - 1 2 3 4 5 6 7 8 9 10 11 12 13 14 15

#anote2self

DATE: / / ◑ TIME :

DO YOU DO MORE HARM TO YOURSELF THAN GOOD?

DEAR SELF,

MY INTENTIONS FOR TODAY ARE

1.
2.
3.

I AM THANKFUL FOR

I WILL ACCOMPLISH THESE THINGS TODAY

1.
2.
3.

I AM GOING TO ENJOY

1.
2.
3.

I NEED TO WORK ON

1.
2.

min - *1   2   3   4   5   6   7   8   9   10   11   12   13   14   15*

#anote2self

DATE: / / TIME :

DO YOU DEPEND TOO MUCH ON OUTSIDE SOURCES TO MAKE YOU HAPPY?

DEAR SELF,

MY INTENTIONS FOR TODAY ARE

1.
2.
3.

I AM THANKFUL FOR

I WILL ACCOMPLISH THESE THINGS TODAY

1.
2.
3.

I AM GOING TO ENJOY

1.
2.
3.

I NEED TO WORK ON

1.
2.

min - 1 2 3 4 5 6 7 8 9 10 11 12 13 14 15

#anote2self

DATE: /   /   ◗   TIME   :

HOW DOES MEDITATION NURTURE YOUR SPIRITUALITY?

DEAR SELF,

MY INTENTIONS FOR TODAY ARE

1.
2.
3.

I AM THANKFUL FOR

I WILL ACCOMPLISH THESE THINGS TODAY

1.
2.
3.

I AM GOING TO ENJOY

1.
2.
3.

I NEED TO WORK ON

1.
2.

min - 1   2   3   4   5   6   7   8   9   10   11   12   13   14   15

#anote2self

DATE: /   /   ◐   TIME   :

DESCRIBE YOUR PURSUIT OF HAPPINESS.

_____
_____
_____
_____

DEAR SELF,

_____
_____
_____
_____

MY INTENTIONS FOR TODAY ARE

1. _____
2. _____
3. _____

I AM THANKFUL FOR

_____

I WILL ACCOMPLISH THESE THINGS TODAY

1. _____
2. _____
3. _____

I AM GOING TO ENJOY

1. _____
2. _____
3. _____

I NEED TO WORK ON

1. _____
2. _____

min - 1   2   3   4   5   6   7   8   9   10   11   12   13   14   15

#anote2self

DATE: / / ◗ TIME :

HOW IS INSTANT GRATIFICATION DIFFERENT FROM SELF-LOVE?

DEAR SELF,

MY INTENTIONS FOR TODAY ARE

1.
2.
3.

I AM THANKFUL FOR

I WILL ACCOMPLISH THESE THINGS TODAY

1.
2.
3.

I AM GOING TO ENJOY

1.
2.
3.

I NEED TO WORK ON

1.
2.

min - *1 2 3 4 5 6 7 8 9 10 11 12 13 14 15*

#anote2self

DATE: / /   TIME   :

HOW CAN YOU PREVENT YOUR HAPPINESS FROM SHIFTING WHEN PRESENTED WITH OBSTRUCTIONS?

DEAR SELF,

MY INTENTIONS FOR TODAY ARE

1.
2.
3.

I AM THANKFUL FOR

I WILL ACCOMPLISH THESE THINGS TODAY

1.
2.
3.

I AM GOING TO ENJOY

1.
2.
3.

I NEED TO WORK ON

1.
2.

min - 1 2 3 4 5 6 7 8 9 10 11 12 13 14 15

#anote2self

DATE: / /   TIME :

CAN YOU FIND HAPPINESS WITHOUT FIRST LOVING YOURSELF? WHY OR WHY NOT?

DEAR SELF,

MY INTENTIONS FOR TODAY ARE

1.
2.
3.

I AM THANKFUL FOR

I WILL ACCOMPLISH THESE THINGS TODAY

1.
2.
3.

I AM GOING TO ENJOY

1.
2.
3.

I NEED TO WORK ON

1.
2.

min - 1 2 3 4 5 6 7 8 9 10 11 12 13 14 15

#anote2self

DATE: / / ◯ TIME :

WHAT PURPOSE CAN NATURE SERVE WHEN IT COMES TO LEARNING SELF-LOVE?

_____
_____
_____
_____

DEAR SELF,

_____
_____
_____

MY INTENTIONS FOR TODAY ARE

1. _____
2. _____
3. _____

I AM THANKFUL FOR

_____

I WILL ACCOMPLISH THESE THINGS TODAY

1. _____
2. _____
3. _____

I AM GOING TO ENJOY

1. _____
2. _____
3. _____

I NEED TO WORK ON

1. _____
2. _____

min - _1 2 3 4 5 6 7 8 9 10 11 12 13 14 15_

#anote2self

DATE: / / TIME :

IS SELF-LOVE SOMETHING THAT WE CAN LEARN?

DEAR SELF,

MY INTENTIONS FOR TODAY ARE

1.
2.
3.

I AM THANKFUL FOR

I WILL ACCOMPLISH THESE THINGS TODAY

1.
2.
3.

I AM GOING TO ENJOY

1.
2.
3.

I NEED TO WORK ON

1.
2.

DATE: /   /   TIME   :

WHAT ARE SOME OF THE BEST LESSONS YOU HAVE TAUGHT YOURSELF OVER
THE PAST YEAR?

DEAR SELF,

MY INTENTIONS FOR TODAY ARE

1.
2.
3.

I AM THANKFUL FOR

I WILL ACCOMPLISH THESE THINGS TODAY

1.
2.
3.

I AM GOING TO ENJOY

1.
2.
3.

I NEED TO WORK ON

1.
2.

min - 1   2   3   4   5   6   7   8   9   10   11   12   13   14   15

#anote2self

DATE: /   /   ◑   TIME   :

DESCRIBE WHAT SELF-PRESERVATION MEANS TO YOU.

DEAR SELF,

MY INTENTIONS FOR TODAY ARE

1.
2.
3.

I AM THANKFUL FOR

I WILL ACCOMPLISH THESE THINGS TODAY

1.
2.
3.

I AM GOING TO ENJOY

1.
2.
3.

I NEED TO WORK ON

1.
2.

min - 1   2   3   4   5   6   7   8   9   10   11   12   13   14   15

#anote2self

DATE: /   /   ◖   TIME   :

HOW CAN SELF-LOVE AID IN MAINTAINING RELATIONSHIPS?

DEAR SELF,

MY INTENTIONS FOR TODAY ARE

1.
2.
3.

I AM THANKFUL FOR

I WILL ACCOMPLISH THESE THINGS TODAY

1.
2.
3.

I AM GOING TO ENJOY

1.
2.
3.

I NEED TO WORK ON

1.
2.

min - *1   2   3   4   5   6   7   8   9   10   11   12   13   14   15*

#anote2self

DATE: /   /   ◑   TIME   :

WHAT DO YOU THINK ARE THE MAJOR INGREDIENTS FOR HAPPINESS?

DEAR SELF,

MY INTENTIONS FOR TODAY ARE

1.
2.
3.

I AM THANKFUL FOR

I WILL ACCOMPLISH THESE THINGS TODAY

1.
2.
3.

I AM GOING TO ENJOY

1.
2.
3.

I NEED TO WORK ON

1.
2.

min - 1   2   3   4   5   6   7   8   9   10   11   12   13   14   15

#anote2self

DATE: /   /   ◑   TIME   :

TO WHICH ELEMENT—EARTH, AIR, FIRE, OR WATER—ARE YOU MOST DRAWN? WHY?

DEAR SELF,

MY INTENTIONS FOR TODAY ARE

1.
2.
3.

I AM THANKFUL FOR

I WILL ACCOMPLISH THESE THINGS TODAY

1.
2.
3.

I AM GOING TO ENJOY

1.
2.
3.

I NEED TO WORK ON

1.
2.

min - 1   2   3   4   5   6   7   8   9   10   11   12   13   14   15

#anote2self

DO YOU FOCUS TOO MUCH ON YOUR WEAKNESSES AS OPPOSED
TO YOUR STRENGTHS?

DEAR SELF,

MY INTENTIONS FOR TODAY ARE

1.
2.
3.

I AM THANKFUL FOR

I WILL ACCOMPLISH THESE THINGS TODAY

1.
2.
3.

I AM GOING TO ENJOY

1.
2.
3.

I NEED TO WORK ON

1.
2.

DATE: /   /   TIME   :

IF YOU WERE FALLING, HOW WOULD YOU PICK YOURSELF UP?

_____
_____
_____
_____

DEAR SELF,

_____
_____
_____
_____

MY INTENTIONS FOR TODAY ARE

1. _____
2. _____
3. _____

I AM THANKFUL FOR

_____

I WILL ACCOMPLISH THESE THINGS TODAY

1. _____
2. _____
3. _____

I AM GOING TO ENJOY

1. _____
2. _____
3. _____

I NEED TO WORK ON

1. _____
2. _____

min - 1   2   3   4   5   6   7   8   9   10   11   12   13   14   15

#anote2self

DATE: / / 🌗 TIME :

DESCRIBE YOUR SUPPORT SYSTEM AND HOW IT INSPIRES YOU.

_____
_____
_____
_____

DEAR SELF,

_____
_____
_____
_____

MY INTENTIONS FOR TODAY ARE

1. _____
2. _____
3. _____

I AM THANKFUL FOR

_____

I WILL ACCOMPLISH THESE THINGS TODAY

1. _____
2. _____
3. _____

I AM GOING TO ENJOY

1. _____
2. _____
3. _____

I NEED TO WORK ON

1. _____
2. _____

min - *1 2 3 4 5 6 7 8 9 10 11 12 13 14 15*

DATE: / /   ◐   TIME   :

CAN YOU RECOGNIZE AND ADMIT WHEN YOU NEED HELP?

_____
_____
_____
_____
_____

DEAR SELF,

_____
_____
_____
_____

MY INTENTIONS FOR TODAY ARE

1. _____
2. _____
3. _____

I AM THANKFUL FOR

_____

I WILL ACCOMPLISH THESE THINGS TODAY

1. _____
2. _____
3. _____

I AM GOING TO ENJOY

1. _____
2. _____
3. _____

I NEED TO WORK ON

1. _____
2. _____

min - *1   2   3   4   5   6   7   8   9   10   11   12   13   14   15*

#anote2self

DATE: / /   ●   TIME :

ARE YOU HOLDING ON TO TOXIC RELATIONSHIPS? IF SO, WHY?

DEAR SELF,

MY INTENTIONS FOR TODAY ARE

1.
2.
3.

I AM THANKFUL FOR

I WILL ACCOMPLISH THESE THINGS TODAY

1.
2.
3.

I AM GOING TO ENJOY

1.
2.
3.

I NEED TO WORK ON

1.
2.

min - 1   2   3   4   5   6   7   8   9   10   11   12   13   14   15

#anote2self

DATE: /   /   ●   TIME   :

WHAT BURDENS DO YOU CARRY? HOW CAN YOU RELEASE THEM?

DEAR SELF,

MY INTENTIONS FOR TODAY ARE

1.
2.
3.

I AM THANKFUL FOR

I WILL ACCOMPLISH THESE THINGS TODAY

1.
2.
3.

I AM GOING TO ENJOY

1.
2.
3.

I NEED TO WORK ON

1.
2.

min - 1   2   3   4   5   6   7   8   9   10   11   12   13   14   15

#anote2self

"LOVE IS TO BE SHARED NOT SHELTERED OR HOARDED.
CHANGE A LIFE WITH WITH YOUR STORIES, JOY & BLESSINGS"

DATE: / /   ⬤   TIME :

HOW DO YOU INSPIRE THE PEOPLE AROUND YOU?

DEAR SELF,

MY INTENTIONS FOR TODAY ARE

1.
2.
3.

I AM THANKFUL FOR

I WILL ACCOMPLISH THESE THINGS TODAY

1.
2.
3.

I AM GOING TO ENJOY

1.
2.
3.

I NEED TO WORK ON

1.
2.

min - 1 2 3 4 5 6 7 8 9 10 11 12 13 14 15

#anote2self

DATE: /   /   ●   TIME   :

DO YOU FORGIVE YOURSELF FOR THE MISTAKES YOU'VE MADE IN YOUR PAST?

DEAR SELF,

MY INTENTIONS FOR TODAY ARE

1.
2.
3.

I AM THANKFUL FOR

I WILL ACCOMPLISH THESE THINGS TODAY

1.
2.
3.

I AM GOING TO ENJOY

1.
2.
3.

I NEED TO WORK ON

1.
2.

min - 1   2   3   4   5   6   7   8   9   10   11   12   13   14   15

#anote2self

DATE: /   /   ●   TIME   :

DO YOU HAVE THE ABILITY TO SEE SITUATIONS THROUGH SOMEONE ELSE'S EYE?

DEAR SELF,

MY INTENTIONS FOR TODAY ARE
1.
2.
3.

I AM THANKFUL FOR

I WILL ACCOMPLISH THESE THINGS TODAY
1.
2.
3.

I AM GOING TO ENJOY
1.
2.
3.

I NEED TO WORK ON
1.
2.

min - *1 2 3 4 5 6 7 8 9 10 11 12 13 14 15*

#anote2self

DATE: /   /   ●   TIME   :

IS WHAT YOU PUT INTO YOUR BODY A REFLECTION OF YOUR SELF-WORTH?

DEAR SELF,

MY INTENTIONS FOR TODAY ARE
1.
2.
3.

I AM THANKFUL FOR

I WILL ACCOMPLISH THESE THINGS TODAY
1.
2.
3.

I AM GOING TO ENJOY
1.
2.
3.

I NEED TO WORK ON
1.
2.

min - 1   2   3   4   5   6   7   8   9   10   11   12   13   14   15

#anote2self

DATE: / / TIME :

DO YOU FIND YOUR MIND FORMULATING AN ANSWER BEFORE THE
WHOLE QUESTION IS ASKED?

DEAR SELF,

MY INTENTIONS FOR TODAY ARE

1.
2.
3.

I AM THANKFUL FOR

I WILL ACCOMPLISH THESE THINGS TODAY

1.
2.
3.

I AM GOING TO ENJOY

1.
2.
3.

I NEED TO WORK ON

1.
2.

min - 1 2 3 4 5 6 7 8 9 10 11 12 13 14 15

#anote2self

DATE: /   /   TIME   :

DO YOU BECOME UPSET BY THE LOSS OF THINGS NOT MEANT TO STAY?

_____
_____
_____
_____

DEAR SELF,

_____
_____
_____
_____

MY INTENTIONS FOR TODAY ARE

1. _____
2. _____
3. _____

I AM THANKFUL FOR

_____

I WILL ACCOMPLISH THESE THINGS TODAY

1. _____
2. _____
3. _____

I AM GOING TO ENJOY

1. _____
2. _____
3. _____

I NEED TO WORK ON

1. _____
2. _____

min - 1   2   3   4   5   6   7   8   9   10   11   12   13   14   15

#anote2self

WHICH SIDE OF A SCALE WOULD OUTWEIGH THE OTHER—THE ONE HOLDING
SELF-WORTH OR SELF-DOUBT?

_____
_____
_____

DEAR SELF,

_____
_____
_____
_____

MY INTENTIONS FOR TODAY ARE

1. _____
2. _____
3. _____

I AM THANKFUL FOR

_____

I WILL ACCOMPLISH THESE THINGS TODAY

1. _____
2. _____
3. _____

I AM GOING TO ENJOY

1. _____
2. _____
3. _____

I NEED TO WORK ON

1. _____
2. _____

DATE: /   /   ◑   TIME   :

ARE YOU MORE DRAWN TO THE SUN OR THE MOON?

_____
_____
_____
_____

DEAR SELF,

_____
_____
_____
_____

MY INTENTIONS FOR TODAY ARE

1. _____
2. _____
3. _____

I AM THANKFUL FOR

_____

I WILL ACCOMPLISH THESE THINGS TODAY

1. _____
2. _____
3. _____

I AM GOING TO ENJOY

1. _____
2. _____
3. _____

I NEED TO WORK ON

1. _____
2. _____

DATE: / /

TIME :

HOW DO YOU SAVE YOU MEMORIES?

DEAR SELF,

MY INTENTIONS FOR TODAY ARE

1.
2.
3.

I AM THANKFUL FOR

I WILL ACCOMPLISH THESE THINGS TODAY

1.
2.
3.

I AM GOING TO ENJOY

1.
2.
3.

I NEED TO WORK ON

1.
2.

min - *1 2 3 4 5 6 7 8 9 10 11 12 13 14 15*

#anote2self

DATE: /   /   ◗   TIME   :

WHEN WAS THE LAST TIME YOU TOOK A WALK DOWN MEMORY LANE?

DEAR SELF,

MY INTENTIONS FOR TODAY ARE

1.
2.
3.

I AM THANKFUL FOR

I WILL ACCOMPLISH THESE THINGS TODAY

1.
2.
3.

I AM GOING TO ENJOY

1.
2.
3.

I NEED TO WORK ON

1.
2.

min - 1   2   3   4   5   6   7   8   9   10   11   12   13   14   15

#anote2self

DATE: /   /   ◐   TIME   :

WHAT IS ONE THING YOU'VE ALWAYS LOVED ABOUT YOURSELF?

DEAR SELF,

MY INTENTIONS FOR TODAY ARE

1.
2.
3.

I AM THANKFUL FOR

I WILL ACCOMPLISH THESE THINGS TODAY

1.
2.
3.

I AM GOING TO ENJOY

1.
2.
3.

I NEED TO WORK ON

1.
2.

min - 1 2 3 4 5 6 7 8 9 10 11 12 13 14 15

#anote2self

DATE: /   /   ◗   TIME   :

DO YOU TEND TO LOVE OTHERS MORE THAN YOU LOVE YOURSELF?

_____
_____
_____
_____

DEAR SELF,

_____
_____
_____
_____

MY INTENTIONS FOR TODAY ARE

1. _____
2. _____
3. _____

I AM THANKFUL FOR

_____

I WILL ACCOMPLISH THESE THINGS TODAY

1. _____
2. _____
3. _____

I AM GOING TO ENJOY

1. _____
2. _____
3. _____

I NEED TO WORK ON

1. _____
2. _____

min - 1   2   3   4   5   6   7   8   9   10   11   12   13   14   15

#anote2self

DATE: /   /   ◖   TIME   :

TO WHAT EXTENT IS YOUR SELF-WORTH TIED TO THE OPINIONS OF OTHERS?

DEAR SELF,

MY INTENTIONS FOR TODAY ARE

1.
2.
3.

I AM THANKFUL FOR

I WILL ACCOMPLISH THESE THINGS TODAY

1.
2.
3.

I AM GOING TO ENJOY

1.
2.
3.

I NEED TO WORK ON

1.
2.

min - 1   2   3   4   5   6   7   8   9   10   11   12   13   14   15

#anote2self

DATE: /   /   ◯   TIME   :

HAVE YOU CATERED TO YOURSELF RECENTLY? IF NOT, HOW COME?

DEAR SELF,

MY INTENTIONS FOR TODAY ARE

1.
2.
3.

I AM THANKFUL FOR

I WILL ACCOMPLISH THESE THINGS TODAY

1.
2.
3.

I AM GOING TO ENJOY

1.
2.
3.

I NEED TO WORK ON

1.
2.

min - 1   2   3   4   5   6   7   8   9   10   11   12   13   14   15

#anote2self

DATE: / /   TIME   :

DO YOU HAVE A STRONGER DESIRE FOR OTHERS TO LOVE YOU OR FOR YOU TO LOVE YOURSELF?

DEAR SELF,

MY INTENTIONS FOR TODAY ARE

1.
2.
3.

I AM THANKFUL FOR

I WILL ACCOMPLISH THESE THINGS TODAY

1.
2.
3.

I AM GOING TO ENJOY

1.
2.
3.

I NEED TO WORK ON

1.
2.

min - *1 2 3 4 5 6 7 8 9 10 11 12 13 14 15*

#anote2self

DATE: /   /   ◐   TIME   :

WHAT DISTRACTIONS PREVENT YOU FROM BEING ABLE TO ENJOY THE PRESENT?

DEAR SELF,

MY INTENTIONS FOR TODAY ARE

1.
2.
3.

I AM THANKFUL FOR

I WILL ACCOMPLISH THESE THINGS TODAY

1.
2.
3.

I AM GOING TO ENJOY

1.
2.
3.

I NEED TO WORK ON

1.
2.

min - 1   2   3   4   5   6   7   8   9   10   11   12   13   14   15

#anote2self

DATE: /   /   ◖   TIME   :

WHAT OBSTACLES ARE HOLDING YOU BACK FROM GETTING WHERE YOU NEED TO BE?

DEAR SELF,

MY INTENTIONS FOR TODAY ARE
1.
2.
3.

I AM THANKFUL FOR

I WILL ACCOMPLISH THESE THINGS TODAY
1.
2.
3.

I AM GOING TO ENJOY
1.
2.
3.

I NEED TO WORK ON
1.
2.

min - 1   2   3   4   5   6   7   8   9   10   11   12   13   14   15

#anote2self

DATE: /   /   ◐   TIME   :

WHAT EFFORTS CAN YOU MAKE TO REMOVE THE OBSTACLES THAT HOLD
YOU BACK FROM SUCCESS?

DEAR SELF,

MY INTENTIONS FOR TODAY ARE

1.
2.
3.

I AM THANKFUL FOR

I WILL ACCOMPLISH THESE THINGS TODAY

1.
2.
3.

I AM GOING TO ENJOY

1.
2.
3.

I NEED TO WORK ON

1.
2.

min - 1   2   3   4   5   6   7   8   9   10   11   12   13   14   15

#anote2self

DATE: /   /   ◑   TIME   :

DO YOU HAVE A PLACE OF PEACE?

DEAR SELF,

MY INTENTIONS FOR TODAY ARE

1.
2.
3.

I AM THANKFUL FOR

I WILL ACCOMPLISH THESE THINGS TODAY

1.
2.
3.

I AM GOING TO ENJOY

1.
2.
3.

I NEED TO WORK ON

1.
2.

min - 1   2   3   4   5   6   7   8   9   10   11   12   13   14   15

#anote2self

DATE: / /   ◑   TIME :

ARE YOU TOO WORRIED ABOUT TOMORROW TO FOCUS ON TODAY?

DEAR SELF,

MY INTENTIONS FOR TODAY ARE

1.
2.
3.

I AM THANKFUL FOR

I WILL ACCOMPLISH THESE THINGS TODAY

1.
2.
3.

I AM GOING TO ENJOY

1.
2.
3.

I NEED TO WORK ON

1.
2.

min - 1 2 3 4 5 6 7 8 9 10 11 12 13 14 15

#anote2self

DATE: /   /   ◐   TIME   :

DO YOU MAINTAIN A GOOD BALANCE BETWEEN WORK AND FAMILY LIFE?

DEAR SELF,

MY INTENTIONS FOR TODAY ARE

1.
2.
3.

I AM THANKFUL FOR

I WILL ACCOMPLISH THESE THINGS TODAY

1.
2.
3.

I AM GOING TO ENJOY

1.
2.
3.

I NEED TO WORK ON

1.
2.

min - 1   2   3   4   5   6   7   8   9   10   11   12   13   14   15

#anote2self

DATE: / / TIME :

ARE YOU ABLE TO RECOGNIZE A POTENTIALLY STRESSFUL SITUATION AND HEALTHILY EVADE IT?

DEAR SELF,

MY INTENTIONS FOR TODAY ARE
1.
2.
3.

I AM THANKFUL FOR

I WILL ACCOMPLISH THESE THINGS TODAY
1.
2.
3.

I AM GOING TO ENJOY
1.
2.
3.

I NEED TO WORK ON
1.
2.

min - *1 2 3 4 5 6 7 8 9 10 11 12 13 14 15*

#anote2self

DATE: / / ◑ TIME :

DO YOU TRUST TOO EASILY? TOO RELUCTANTLY?

DEAR SELF,

MY INTENTIONS FOR TODAY ARE

1.
2.
3.

I AM THANKFUL FOR

I WILL ACCOMPLISH THESE THINGS TODAY

1.
2.
3.

I AM GOING TO ENJOY

1.
2.
3.

I NEED TO WORK ON

1.
2.

min - *1 2 3 4 5 6 7 8 9 10 11 12 13 14 15*

#anote2self

DATE: /   /   ◑   TIME   :

WHAT MISCONCEPTIONS DO PEOPLE HAVE ABOUT YOU?
HOW DO YOU WORK TO ERADICATE THEM?

DEAR SELF,

MY INTENTIONS FOR TODAY ARE
1.
2.
3.

I AM THANKFUL FOR

I WILL ACCOMPLISH THESE THINGS TODAY
1.
2.
3.

I AM GOING TO ENJOY
1.
2.
3.

I NEED TO WORK ON
1.
2.

min - 1   2   3   4   5   6   7   8   9   10   11   12   13   14   15
#anote2self

DATE: /   /   ☽   TIME   :

DO YOU HAVE A HARD TIME SAYING NO?

DEAR SELF,

MY INTENTIONS FOR TODAY ARE

1.
2.
3.

I AM THANKFUL FOR

I WILL ACCOMPLISH THESE THINGS TODAY

1.
2.
3.

I AM GOING TO ENJOY

1.
2.
3.

I NEED TO WORK ON

1.
2.

DATE: / / TIME :

ARE YOU MORE CONCERNED WITH PLEASING OTHERS THAN PLEASING YOURSELF?

DEAR SELF,

MY INTENTIONS FOR TODAY ARE
1.
2.
3.

I AM THANKFUL FOR

I WILL ACCOMPLISH THESE THINGS TODAY
1.
2.
3.

I AM GOING TO ENJOY
1.
2.
3.

I NEED TO WORK ON
1.
2.

min - 1 2 3 4 5 6 7 8 9 10 11 12 13 14 15

#anote2self

DATE: / / TIME :

LIST FIVE POSITIVE QUALITIES ABOUT YOURSELF.

DEAR SELF,

MY INTENTIONS FOR TODAY ARE

1.
2.
3.

I AM THANKFUL FOR

I WILL ACCOMPLISH THESE THINGS TODAY

1.
2.
3.

I AM GOING TO ENJOY

1.
2.
3.

I NEED TO WORK ON

1.
2.

min - *1 2 3 4 5 6 7 8 9 10 11 12 13 14 15*

#anote2self

DATE: /   /   ●   TIME   :

IS IT HARD FOR YOU TO LET GO?

DEAR SELF,

MY INTENTIONS FOR TODAY ARE

1.
2.
3.

I AM THANKFUL FOR

I WILL ACCOMPLISH THESE THINGS TODAY

1.
2.
3.

I AM GOING TO ENJOY

1.
2.
3.

I NEED TO WORK ON

1.
2.

min - 1   2   3   4   5   6   7   8   9   10   11   12   13   14   15

#anote2self

"BE PROUD OF YOURSELF. JOURNEY UNASHAMED & FULL OF ACCEPTANCE. EACH LESSON IS A BUILDING BLOCK FOR YOUR SUCCESS."

DATE: /   /   ●   TIME   :

WHEN IS THE LAST TIME YOU CRIED, AND WHY?

_____
_____
_____
_____

DEAR SELF,

_____
_____
_____
_____

MY INTENTIONS FOR TODAY ARE

1. _____
2. _____
3. _____

I AM THANKFUL FOR

_____

I WILL ACCOMPLISH THESE THINGS TODAY

1. _____
2. _____
3. _____

I AM GOING TO ENJOY

1. _____
2. _____
3. _____

I NEED TO WORK ON

1. _____
2. _____

min - _1   2   3   4   5   6   7   8   9   10   11   12   13   14   15_

#anote2self

DATE: /   /   ●   TIME   :

NAME FIVE THINGS THAT MAKE YOU HAPPY.

DEAR SELF,

MY INTENTIONS FOR TODAY ARE
1.
2.
3.

I AM THANKFUL FOR

I WILL ACCOMPLISH THESE THINGS TODAY
1.
2.
3.

I AM GOING TO ENJOY
1.
2.
3.

I NEED TO WORK ON
1.
2.

min - 1   2   3   4   5   6   7   8   9   10   11   12   13   14   15

#anote2self

DATE: / / ● TIME :

DEFINE YOUR PERSONAL CHANGE.

DEAR SELF,

MY INTENTIONS FOR TODAY ARE

1.
2.
3.

I AM THANKFUL FOR

I WILL ACCOMPLISH THESE THINGS TODAY

1.
2.
3.

I AM GOING TO ENJOY

1.
2.
3.

I NEED TO WORK ON

1.
2.

min - 1 2 3 4 5 6 7 8 9 10 11 12 13 14 15

#anote2self

DATE: /   /   ◐   TIME   :

ARE YOU NOT AFRAID TO WALK YOUR OWN PATH?

_____
_____
_____
_____

DEAR SELF,

_____
_____
_____
_____

MY INTENTIONS FOR TODAY ARE

1. _____
2. _____
3. _____

I AM THANKFUL FOR

_____

I WILL ACCOMPLISH THESE THINGS TODAY

1. _____
2. _____
3. _____

I AM GOING TO ENJOY

1. _____
2. _____
3. _____

I NEED TO WORK ON

1. _____
2. _____

min - _1   2   3   4   5   6   7   8   9   10   11   12   13   14   15_

#anote2self

DATE: /   /   ◑   TIME   :

ARE YOU JOURNEYING FREELY?

DEAR SELF,

MY INTENTIONS FOR TODAY ARE

1.
2.
3.

I AM THANKFUL FOR

I WILL ACCOMPLISH THESE THINGS TODAY

1.
2.
3.

I AM GOING TO ENJOY

1.
2.
3.

I NEED TO WORK ON

1.
2.

min - 1   2   3   4   5   6   7   8   9   10   11   12   13   14   15

#anote2self

DATE: /   /   ☽   TIME   :

WHAT WARMS YOUR SOUL AND IGNITES YOUR PASSION?

DEAR SELF,

MY INTENTIONS FOR TODAY ARE

1.
2.
3.

I AM THANKFUL FOR

I WILL ACCOMPLISH THESE THINGS TODAY

1.
2.
3.

I AM GOING TO ENJOY

1.
2.
3.

I NEED TO WORK ON

1.
2.

min - *1   2   3   4   5   6   7   8   9   10   11   12   13   14   15*

#anote2self

DATE: / / TIME :

WHAT QUESTIONS DO YOU ASK YOURSELF EVERYDAY?

DEAR SELF,

MY INTENTIONS FOR TODAY ARE
1.
2.
3.

I AM THANKFUL FOR

I WILL ACCOMPLISH THESE THINGS TODAY
1.
2.
3.

I AM GOING TO ENJOY
1.
2.
3.

I NEED TO WORK ON
1.
2.

min - 1 2 3 4 5 6 7 8 9 10 11 12 13 14 15

#anote2self

DATE: / / TIME :

WHAT MAKES YOU LOVE YOURSELF MORE TODAY THAN YOU HAVE IN THE PAST?

DEAR SELF,

MY INTENTIONS FOR TODAY ARE

1.
2.
3.

I AM THANKFUL FOR

I WILL ACCOMPLISH THESE THINGS TODAY

1.
2.
3.

I AM GOING TO ENJOY

1.
2.
3.

I NEED TO WORK ON

1.
2.

min - 1 2 3 4 5 6 7 8 9 10 11 12 13 14 15

#anote2self

DATE: /   /   ◐   TIME   :

HOW DO YOU PRACTICE PEACEFULNESS?

_____
_____
_____
_____

DEAR SELF,

_____
_____
_____
_____

MY INTENTIONS FOR TODAY ARE

1. _____
2. _____
3. _____

I AM THANKFUL FOR

_____

I WILL ACCOMPLISH THESE THINGS TODAY

1. _____
2. _____
3. _____

I AM GOING TO ENJOY

1. _____
2. _____
3. _____

I NEED TO WORK ON

1. _____
2. _____

min - 1   2   3   4   5   6   7   8   9   10   11   12   13   14   15

#anote2self

DATE: /   /   ◐   TIME   :

WHAT GOOD HABITS MAKE YOU PROUD?

DEAR SELF,

MY INTENTIONS FOR TODAY ARE
1.
2.
3.

I AM THANKFUL FOR

I WILL ACCOMPLISH THESE THINGS TODAY
1.
2.
3.

I AM GOING TO ENJOY
1.
2.
3.

I NEED TO WORK ON
1.
2.

min - 1   2   3   4   5   6   7   8   9   10   11   12   13   14   15

#anote2self

DATE: /   /   ◐   TIME   :

WHAT BAD HABITS DO YOU WANT TO BREAK?

_____
_____
_____
_____

DEAR SELF,

_____
_____
_____
_____

MY INTENTIONS FOR TODAY ARE

1. _____
2. _____
3. _____

I AM THANKFUL FOR

_____

I WILL ACCOMPLISH THESE THINGS TODAY

1. _____
2. _____
3. _____

I AM GOING TO ENJOY

1. _____
2. _____
3. _____

I NEED TO WORK ON

1. _____
2. _____

min - 1   2   3   4   5   6   7   8   9   10   11   12   13   14   15

#anote2self

DATE: /   /   ◐   TIME   :

WHAT MOTIVATES YOU TO DO BETTER TODAY?
WHAT HAS MOTIVATED YOU IN THE PAST?

_____
_____
_____

DEAR SELF,

_____
_____
_____
_____

MY INTENTIONS FOR TODAY ARE

1. _____
2. _____
3. _____

I AM THANKFUL FOR

_____

I WILL ACCOMPLISH THESE THINGS TODAY

1. _____
2. _____
3. _____

I AM GOING TO ENJOY

1. _____
2. _____
3. _____

I NEED TO WORK ON

1. _____
2. _____

DATE: /   /   ◖   TIME   :

ARE YOU FULFILLING YOUR DREAMS? DO YOU SEE A LIGHT AT THE END OF THE TUNNEL?

DEAR SELF,

MY INTENTIONS FOR TODAY ARE

1.
2.
3.

I AM THANKFUL FOR

I WILL ACCOMPLISH THESE THINGS TODAY

1.
2.
3.

I AM GOING TO ENJOY

1.
2.
3.

I NEED TO WORK ON

1.
2.

min - 1   2   3   4   5   6   7   8   9   10   11   12   13   14   15

#anote2self

DATE: / / TIME :

DO YOU PRACTICE DAILY SELF-CARE? IF SO, HOW?

DEAR SELF,

MY INTENTIONS FOR TODAY ARE

1.
2.
3.

I AM THANKFUL FOR

I WILL ACCOMPLISH THESE THINGS TODAY

1.
2.
3.

I AM GOING TO ENJOY

1.
2.
3.

I NEED TO WORK ON

1.
2.

min - 1 2 3 4 5 6 7 8 9 10 11 12 13 14 15

#anote2self

DATE: /   /   ◯   TIME   :

LIST FIVE THINGS THAT YOU ARE GRATEFUL FOR.

DEAR SELF,

MY INTENTIONS FOR TODAY ARE

1.
2.
3.

I AM THANKFUL FOR

I WILL ACCOMPLISH THESE THINGS TODAY

1.
2.
3.

I AM GOING TO ENJOY

1.
2.
3.

I NEED TO WORK ON

1.
2.

min - 1   2   3   4   5   6   7   8   9   10   11   12   13   14   15

#anote2self

DATE: / / ◐ TIME :

DO YOU ACKNOWLEDGE YOUR BLESSINGS DAILY?

_____
_____
_____
_____

DEAR SELF,

_____
_____
_____
_____

MY INTENTIONS FOR TODAY ARE

1. _____
2. _____
3. _____

I AM THANKFUL FOR

_____

I WILL ACCOMPLISH THESE THINGS TODAY

1. _____
2. _____
3. _____

I AM GOING TO ENJOY

1. _____
2. _____
3. _____

I NEED TO WORK ON

1. _____
2. _____

min - 1 2 3 4 5 6 7 8 9 10 11 12 13 14 15

#anote2self

DATE: /   /   ◐   TIME   :

WHAT POSITIVE THOUGHTS HAVE YOU HAD ABOUT YOURSELF RECENTLY?

DEAR SELF,

MY INTENTIONS FOR TODAY ARE
1.
2.
3.

I AM THANKFUL FOR

I WILL ACCOMPLISH THESE THINGS TODAY
1.
2.
3.

I AM GOING TO ENJOY
1.
2.
3.

I NEED TO WORK ON
1.
2.

min - 1   2   3   4   5   6   7   8   9   10   11   12   13   14   15

#anote2self

DATE: /   /   ◑   TIME   :

WHEN IS THE LAST TIME YOU REWARDED YOURSELF FOR SOMETHING
YOU HAVE ACHIEVED?

DEAR SELF,

MY INTENTIONS FOR TODAY ARE
1.
2.
3.

I AM THANKFUL FOR

I WILL ACCOMPLISH THESE THINGS TODAY
1.
2.
3.

I AM GOING TO ENJOY
1.
2.
3.

I NEED TO WORK ON
1.
2.

min - 1   2   3   4   5   6   7   8   9   10   11   12   13   14   15
#anote2self

DATE: / / ◑ TIME :

ARE YOU STILL DISCOVERING PARTS OF YOURSELF? WHAT PART OF YOURSELF
MOST INTERESTS YOU?

DEAR SELF,

MY INTENTIONS FOR TODAY ARE

1.
2.
3.

I AM THANKFUL FOR

I WILL ACCOMPLISH THESE THINGS TODAY

1.
2.
3.

I AM GOING TO ENJOY

1.
2.
3.

I NEED TO WORK ON

1.
2.

min - *1* *2* *3* *4* *5* *6* *7* *8* *9* *10* *11* *12* *13* *14* *15*

#anote2self

DATE: /   /   ◑   TIME   :

DO YOU NURTURE HEALTHY RELATIONSHIPS AND REMOVE UNHEALTHY ONES?
_____
_____
_____
_____

DEAR SELF,
_____
_____
_____
_____

MY INTENTIONS FOR TODAY ARE
1. _____
2. _____
3. _____

I AM THANKFUL FOR
_____

I WILL ACCOMPLISH THESE THINGS TODAY
1. _____
2. _____
3. _____

I AM GOING TO ENJOY
1. _____
2. _____
3. _____

I NEED TO WORK ON
1. _____
2. _____

min - 1   2   3   4   5   6   7   8   9   10   11   12   13   14   15

#anote2self

DATE: / / TIME :

HOW DOES IT FEEL TO DO NICE THINGS FOR OTHERS?

DEAR SELF,

MY INTENTIONS FOR TODAY ARE
1.
2.
3.

I AM THANKFUL FOR

I WILL ACCOMPLISH THESE THINGS TODAY
1.
2.
3.

I AM GOING TO ENJOY
1.
2.
3.

I NEED TO WORK ON
1.
2.

min - *1 2 3 4 5 6 7 8 9 10 11 12 13 14 15*

#anote2self

DATE: / /   ◐   TIME :

ARE YOU USING YOUR TIME IN THE WISEST WAY TO ACHIEVE THE
THINGS YOU WANT?

DEAR SELF,

MY INTENTIONS FOR TODAY ARE

1.
2.
3.

I AM THANKFUL FOR

I WILL ACCOMPLISH THESE THINGS TODAY

1.
2.
3.

I AM GOING TO ENJOY

1.
2.
3.

I NEED TO WORK ON

1.
2.

min - 1 2 3 4 5 6 7 8 9 10 11 12 13 14 15

#anote2self

DATE: / / ◑ TIME :

DO YOU TAKE ANYTHING FOR GRANTED IN YOUR DAILY LIFE?

DEAR SELF,

MY INTENTIONS FOR TODAY ARE

1.
2.
3.

I AM THANKFUL FOR

I WILL ACCOMPLISH THESE THINGS TODAY

1.
2.
3.

I AM GOING TO ENJOY

1.
2.
3.

I NEED TO WORK ON

1.
2.

min - 1 2 3 4 5 6 7 8 9 10 11 12 13 14 15

#anote2self

DATE: /   /   ◑   TIME   :

WERE YOU TRUE TO YOUR BELIEFS WHEN MAKING YOUR LAST BIG DECISION?

DEAR SELF,

MY INTENTIONS FOR TODAY ARE

1.
2.
3.

I AM THANKFUL FOR

I WILL ACCOMPLISH THESE THINGS TODAY

1.
2.
3.

I AM GOING TO ENJOY

1.
2.
3.

I NEED TO WORK ON

1.
2.

min - 1   2   3   4   5   6   7   8   9   10   11   12   13   14   15

#anote2self

DATE: /   /   TIME   :

ARE YOU RECOGNIZING AND TAKING CARE OF YOUR PHYSICAL NEEDS?

DEAR SELF,

MY INTENTIONS FOR TODAY ARE

1.
2.
3.

I AM THANKFUL FOR

I WILL ACCOMPLISH THESE THINGS TODAY

1.
2.
3.

I AM GOING TO ENJOY

1.
2.
3.

I NEED TO WORK ON

1.
2.

min - 1   2   3   4   5   6   7   8   9   10   11   12   13   14   15

#anote2self

DATE: /   /   ◐   TIME   :

ARE YOU ACKNOWLEDGING YOUR SPIRITUAL NEEDS?

_____
_____
_____
_____

DEAR SELF,

_____
_____
_____
_____

MY INTENTIONS FOR TODAY ARE

1. _____
2. _____
3. _____

I AM THANKFUL FOR

_____

I WILL ACCOMPLISH THESE THINGS TODAY

1. _____
2. _____
3. _____

I AM GOING TO ENJOY

1. _____
2. _____
3. _____

I NEED TO WORK ON

1. _____
2. _____

min - 1   2   3   4   5   6   7   8   9   10   11   12   13   14   15

#anote2self

DATE: / / TIME :

ARE YOU LETTING OTHERS CONTROL YOUR PERSPECTIVE?

DEAR SELF,

MY INTENTIONS FOR TODAY ARE
1.
2.
3.

I AM THANKFUL FOR

I WILL ACCOMPLISH THESE THINGS TODAY
1.
2.
3.

I AM GOING TO ENJOY
1.
2.
3.

I NEED TO WORK ON
1.
2.

min - 1 2 3 4 5 6 7 8 9 10 11 12 13 14 15

#anote2self

DATE: /   /   ● TIME   :

DO YOU LET THINGS OUT OF YOUR CONTROL STRESS YOU?

DEAR SELF,

MY INTENTIONS FOR TODAY ARE
1.
2.
3.

I AM THANKFUL FOR

I WILL ACCOMPLISH THESE THINGS TODAY
1.
2.
3.

I AM GOING TO ENJOY
1.
2.
3.

I NEED TO WORK ON
1.
2.

min - 1 2 3 4 5 6 7 8 9 10 11 12 13 14 15

#anote2self

"BELIEVE IN YOUR ABILITIES TO DO WHATEVER IT MAY BE THAT SETTLES

INTO YOUR HEART"

DATE: /   /   ●   TIME   :

ARE YOU ACHIEVING THE SMALL GOALS YOU SET FOR YOURSELF?

DEAR SELF,

MY INTENTIONS FOR TODAY ARE

1.
2.
3.

I AM THANKFUL FOR

I WILL ACCOMPLISH THESE THINGS TODAY

1.
2.
3.

I AM GOING TO ENJOY

1.
2.
3.

I NEED TO WORK ON

1.
2.

min - 1   2   3   4   5   6   7   8   9   10   11   12   13   14   15

#anote2self

DATE: /   /   ●   TIME   :

DO YOU SPREAD YOURSELF TOO THIN?

_____
_____
_____
_____

DEAR SELF,

_____
_____
_____
_____

MY INTENTIONS FOR TODAY ARE

1. _____
2. _____
3. _____

I AM THANKFUL FOR

_____

I WILL ACCOMPLISH THESE THINGS TODAY

1. _____
2. _____
3. _____

I AM GOING TO ENJOY

1. _____
2. _____
3. _____

I NEED TO WORK ON

1. _____
2. _____

min - 1   2   3   4   5   6   7   8   9   10   11   12   13   14   15

#anote2self

DATE: /   /   ●   TIME   :

WHAT KEEPS YOU AWAKE AT NIGHT?

DEAR SELF,

MY INTENTIONS FOR TODAY ARE
1.
2.
3.

I AM THANKFUL FOR

I WILL ACCOMPLISH THESE THINGS TODAY
1.
2.
3.

I AM GOING TO ENJOY
1.
2.
3.

I NEED TO WORK ON
1.
2.

min -   1   2   3   4   5   6   7   8   9   10   11   12   13   14   15

#anote2self

DATE: / / TIME :

WHAT DO YOU FIND YOURSELF DAYDREAMING ABOUT?

DEAR SELF,

MY INTENTIONS FOR TODAY ARE
1.
2.
3.

I AM THANKFUL FOR

I WILL ACCOMPLISH THESE THINGS TODAY
1.
2.
3.

I AM GOING TO ENJOY
1.
2.
3.

I NEED TO WORK ON
1.
2.

min - *1 2 3 4 5 6 7 8 9 10 11 12 13 14 15*

#anote2self

DO YOU HAVE UNREALISTIC EXPECTATIONS OF YOURSELF?

DEAR SELF,

MY INTENTIONS FOR TODAY ARE

1.
2.
3.

I AM THANKFUL FOR

I WILL ACCOMPLISH THESE THINGS TODAY

1.
2.
3.

I AM GOING TO ENJOY

1.
2.
3.

I NEED TO WORK ON

1.
2.

DATE: /   /   ◐   TIME   :

DO YOU WANT TO STAND OUT OR BLEND IN?

_____
_____
_____
_____

DEAR SELF,

_____
_____
_____
_____

MY INTENTIONS FOR TODAY ARE

1. _____
2. _____
3. _____

I AM THANKFUL FOR

_____

I WILL ACCOMPLISH THESE THINGS TODAY

1. _____
2. _____
3. _____

I AM GOING TO ENJOY

1. _____
2. _____
3. _____

I NEED TO WORK ON

1. _____
2. _____

min - _1   2   3   4   5   6   7   8   9   10   11   12   13   14   15_

#anote2self

DATE: / / TIME :

HOW BIG IS YOUR HEART? HOW DO YOU WANT TO EXPAND IT?

DEAR SELF,

MY INTENTIONS FOR TODAY ARE

1.
2.
3.

I AM THANKFUL FOR

I WILL ACCOMPLISH THESE THINGS TODAY

1.
2.
3.

I AM GOING TO ENJOY

1.
2.
3.

I NEED TO WORK ON

1.
2.

min - 1 2 3 4 5 6 7 8 9 10 11 12 13 14 15

#anote2self

DATE: / / TIME :

HOW OPEN IS YOUR MIND? HOW DO YOU WANT TO EXPAND IT?

DEAR SELF,

MY INTENTIONS FOR TODAY ARE

1.
2.
3.

I AM THANKFUL FOR

I WILL ACCOMPLISH THESE THINGS TODAY

1.
2.
3.

I AM GOING TO ENJOY

1.
2.
3.

I NEED TO WORK ON

1.
2.

min - *1 2 3 4 5 6 7 8 9 10 11 12 13 14 15*

#anote2self

HOW DO YOU PROCESS NEGATIVE EMOTIONS?

DEAR SELF,

MY INTENTIONS FOR TODAY ARE

1.
2.
3.

I AM THANKFUL FOR

I WILL ACCOMPLISH THESE THINGS TODAY

1.
2.
3.

I AM GOING TO ENJOY

1.
2.
3.

I NEED TO WORK ON

1.
2.

min - 1   2   3   4   5   6   7   8   9   10   11   12   13   14   15

DATE: /   /   ◖   TIME   :

DO YOU EMBRACE YOUR FLAWS?

_____
_____
_____
_____

DEAR SELF,

_____
_____
_____
_____

MY INTENTIONS FOR TODAY ARE

1. _____
2. _____
3. _____

I AM THANKFUL FOR

_____

I WILL ACCOMPLISH THESE THINGS TODAY

1. _____
2. _____
3. _____

I AM GOING TO ENJOY

1. _____
2. _____
3. _____

I NEED TO WORK ON

1. _____
2. _____

min - 1   2   3   4   5   6   7   8   9   10   11   12   13   14   15

#anote2self

DATE: / /   ◐   TIME :

DEFINE LETTING GO.

DEAR SELF,

MY INTENTIONS FOR TODAY ARE

1.
2.
3.

I AM THANKFUL FOR

I WILL ACCOMPLISH THESE THINGS TODAY

1.
2.
3.

I AM GOING TO ENJOY

1.
2.
3.

I NEED TO WORK ON

1.
2.

min - *1 2 3 4 5 6 7 8 9 10 11 12 13 14 15*

#anote2self

DATE: /   /   ◖   TIME   :

HAVE YOU ENJOYED BEING ALONE LATELY?

DEAR SELF,

MY INTENTIONS FOR TODAY ARE

1.
2.
3.

I AM THANKFUL FOR

I WILL ACCOMPLISH THESE THINGS TODAY

1.
2.
3.

I AM GOING TO ENJOY

1.
2.
3.

I NEED TO WORK ON

1.
2.

min - 1   2   3   4   5   6   7   8   9   10   11   12   13   14   15

#anote2self

DATE: /   /   ◖   TIME   :

HAVE YOU FELT ACCOMPLISHED LATELY?

DEAR SELF,

MY INTENTIONS FOR TODAY ARE

1.
2.
3.

I AM THANKFUL FOR

I WILL ACCOMPLISH THESE THINGS TODAY

1.
2.
3.

I AM GOING TO ENJOY

1.
2.
3.

I NEED TO WORK ON

1.
2.

min - 1   2   3   4   5   6   7   8   9   10   11   12   13   14   15

#anote2self

DATE: / / TIME :

IN WHAT WAYS HAS SPIRITUALITY HELPED YOU?

DEAR SELF,

MY INTENTIONS FOR TODAY ARE

1.
2.
3.

I AM THANKFUL FOR

I WILL ACCOMPLISH THESE THINGS TODAY

1.
2.
3.

I AM GOING TO ENJOY

1.
2.
3.

I NEED TO WORK ON

1.
2.

min - 1 2 3 4 5 6 7 8 9 10 11 12 13 14 15

#anote2self

DATE: / /   TIME :

WHEN DID YOU KNOW YOU HAD TO EMBARK ON THE QUEST TO FIND SELF-LOVE?

DEAR SELF,

MY INTENTIONS FOR TODAY ARE

1.
2.
3.

I AM THANKFUL FOR

I WILL ACCOMPLISH THESE THINGS TODAY

1.
2.
3.

I AM GOING TO ENJOY

1.
2.
3.

I NEED TO WORK ON

1.
2.

min - *1 2 3 4 5 6 7 8 9 10 11 12 13 14 15*

#anote2self

DATE: /   /   ◯   TIME   :

HOW DO YOU COMFORT OTHERS?

DEAR SELF,

MY INTENTIONS FOR TODAY ARE
1.
2.
3.

I AM THANKFUL FOR

I WILL ACCOMPLISH THESE THINGS TODAY
1.
2.
3.

I AM GOING TO ENJOY
1.
2.
3.

I NEED TO WORK ON
1.
2.

min - 1   2   3   4   5   6   7   8   9   10   11   12   13   14   15

#anote2self

DATE: / / ☾ TIME :

HOW CAN PEOPLE IMPROVE THEIR OVERALL OUTLOOKS OF THE WORLD?

DEAR SELF,

MY INTENTIONS FOR TODAY ARE
1.
2.
3.

I AM THANKFUL FOR

I WILL ACCOMPLISH THESE THINGS TODAY
1.
2.
3.

I AM GOING TO ENJOY
1.
2.
3.

I NEED TO WORK ON
1.
2.

min - 1 2 3 4 5 6 7 8 9 10 11 12 13 14 15

#anote2self

DATE: / /

TIME :

WHAT DOES YOUR MEDITATION LOOK LIKE?

DEAR SELF,

MY INTENTIONS FOR TODAY ARE

1.
2.
3.

I AM THANKFUL FOR

I WILL ACCOMPLISH THESE THINGS TODAY

1.
2.
3.

I AM GOING TO ENJOY

1.
2.
3.

I NEED TO WORK ON

1.
2.

min - 1 2 3 4 5 6 7 8 9 10 11 12 13 14 15

#anote2self

DATE: /   /   ◑   TIME   :

ARE YOU PROGRESSING IN YOUR HEALING? IF SO, HOW?

DEAR SELF,

MY INTENTIONS FOR TODAY ARE
1.
2.
3.

I AM THANKFUL FOR

I WILL ACCOMPLISH THESE THINGS TODAY
1.
2.
3.

I AM GOING TO ENJOY
1.
2.
3.

I NEED TO WORK ON
1.
2.

min - 1   2   3   4   5   6   7   8   9   10   11   12   13   14   15

#anote2self

DATE: / / TIME :

HOW HAS YOUR HEART HEALED?

DEAR SELF,

MY INTENTIONS FOR TODAY ARE
1.
2.
3.

I AM THANKFUL FOR

I WILL ACCOMPLISH THESE THINGS TODAY
1.
2.
3.

I AM GOING TO ENJOY
1.
2.
3.

I NEED TO WORK ON
1.
2.

min - *1* *2* *3* *4* *5* *6* *7* *8* *9* *10* *11* *12* *13* *14* *15*

#anote2self

DATE: / / ☽ TIME :

WITH WHAT KIND OF ENERGY SHOULD YOU SURROUND YOURSELF?

DEAR SELF,

MY INTENTIONS FOR TODAY ARE

1.
2.
3.

I AM THANKFUL FOR

I WILL ACCOMPLISH THESE THINGS TODAY

1.
2.
3.

I AM GOING TO ENJOY

1.
2.
3.

I NEED TO WORK ON

1.
2.

min - 1 2 3 4 5 6 7 8 9 10 11 12 13 14 15

#anote2self

DATE: /   /   ◑   TIME   :

WHAT EVERYDAY GOALS SHOULD YOU SET IN ORDER TO EMPOWER YOURSELF?

DEAR SELF,

MY INTENTIONS FOR TODAY ARE
1.
2.
3.

I AM THANKFUL FOR

I WILL ACCOMPLISH THESE THINGS TODAY
1.
2.
3.

I AM GOING TO ENJOY
1.
2.
3.

I NEED TO WORK ON
1.
2.

min - 1   2   3   4   5   6   7   8   9   10   11   12   13   14   15

#anote2self

DATE: / /   ◐   TIME   :

OF WHAT THINGS ARE YOU IN DENIAL?

DEAR SELF,

MY INTENTIONS FOR TODAY ARE

1.
2.
3.

I AM THANKFUL FOR

I WILL ACCOMPLISH THESE THINGS TODAY

1.
2.
3.

I AM GOING TO ENJOY

1.
2.
3.

I NEED TO WORK ON

1.
2.

min - *1   2   3   4   5   6   7   8   9   10   11   12   13   14   15*

#anote2self

DATE: / / TIME :

HOW CAN PEOPLE ACCEPT THEIR PAST TO REINVENT THEMSELVES FOR THE FUTURE?

DEAR SELF,

MY INTENTIONS FOR TODAY ARE
1.
2.
3.

I AM THANKFUL FOR

I WILL ACCOMPLISH THESE THINGS TODAY
1.
2.
3.

I AM GOING TO ENJOY
1.
2.
3.

I NEED TO WORK ON
1.
2.

min - 1 2 3 4 5 6 7 8 9 10 11 12 13 14 15

#anote2self

DATE: / / TIME :

CAN YOU FIND PEACE IN PAIN?

DEAR SELF,

MY INTENTIONS FOR TODAY ARE
1.
2.
3.

I AM THANKFUL FOR

I WILL ACCOMPLISH THESE THINGS TODAY
1.
2.
3.

I AM GOING TO ENJOY
1.
2.
3.

I NEED TO WORK ON
1.
2.

min - 1 2 3 4 5 6 7 8 9 10 11 12 13 14 15

#anote2self

DATE: / /   TIME :

HOW DO YOU CLEAR YOUR MIND WHEN OVER THINKING KICKS IN?

DEAR SELF,

MY INTENTIONS FOR TODAY ARE
1.
2.
3.

I AM THANKFUL FOR

I WILL ACCOMPLISH THESE THINGS TODAY
1.
2.
3.

I AM GOING TO ENJOY
1.
2.
3.

I NEED TO WORK ON
1.
2.

min - 1 2 3 4 5 6 7 8 9 10 11 12 13 14 15

#anote2self

DATE: / /   ●   TIME :

WHERE IS YOUR PLACE OF PEACE?

DEAR SELF,

MY INTENTIONS FOR TODAY ARE

1.
2.
3.

I AM THANKFUL FOR

I WILL ACCOMPLISH THESE THINGS TODAY

1.
2.
3.

I AM GOING TO ENJOY

1.
2.
3.

I NEED TO WORK ON

1.
2.

min - 1 2 3 4 5 6 7 8 9 10 11 12 13 14 15

#anote2self

DATE: / /   ●   TIME :

HOW WELL DO YOU ACCEPT CRITICISM?

DEAR SELF,

MY INTENTIONS FOR TODAY ARE

1.
2.
3.

I AM THANKFUL FOR

I WILL ACCOMPLISH THESE THINGS TODAY

1.
2.
3.

I AM GOING TO ENJOY

1.
2.
3.

I NEED TO WORK ON

1.
2.

min - 1 2 3 4 5 6 7 8 9 10 11 12 13 14 15

#anote2self

"IF YOUR INTENTIONS ARE NOT PURE YOUR ENERGY WILL PROVE
THAT POINT. MAKE SURE YOU ARE WALKING IN YOUR
TRUTH & POSITIVE HIGH VIBRATIONS"

WHAT ARE PHRASES THAT YOU SHOULD SAY TO YOURSELF
WHEN FEELING DISCOURAGED?

DEAR SELF,

MY INTENTIONS FOR TODAY ARE

1.
2.
3.

I AM THANKFUL FOR

I WILL ACCOMPLISH THESE THINGS TODAY

1.
2.
3.

I AM GOING TO ENJOY

1.
2.
3.

I NEED TO WORK ON

1.
2.

min - 1 2 3 4 5 6 7 8 9 10 11 12 13 14 15

#anote2self

DATE: /   /   ●   TIME   :

IS SELF-LOVE AND HEALING SOMETHING THAT TAKES A LONG PERIOD TO PERFECT?

DEAR SELF,

MY INTENTIONS FOR TODAY ARE
1.
2.
3.

I AM THANKFUL FOR

I WILL ACCOMPLISH THESE THINGS TODAY
1.
2.
3.

I AM GOING TO ENJOY
1.
2.
3.

I NEED TO WORK ON
1.
2.

min - 1   2   3   4   5   6   7   8   9   10   11   12   13   14   15

#anote2self

DATE: /   /   ●   TIME   :

WHAT COMFORTS YOU WHEN YOU'RE FEELING DISCOURAGED?

DEAR SELF,

MY INTENTIONS FOR TODAY ARE
1.
2.
3.

I AM THANKFUL FOR

I WILL ACCOMPLISH THESE THINGS TODAY
1.
2.
3.

I AM GOING TO ENJOY
1.
2.
3.

I NEED TO WORK ON
1.
2.

min - 1   2   3   4   5   6   7   8   9   10   11   12   13   14   15

#anote2self

DATE: /   /   ◐   TIME   :

HOW CAN A PERSON BEGIN TO ESTABLISH SOLID TRUST IN ONESELF?

_____
_____
_____
_____

DEAR SELF,

_____
_____
_____
_____

MY INTENTIONS FOR TODAY ARE

1. _____
2. _____
3. _____

I AM THANKFUL FOR

_____

I WILL ACCOMPLISH THESE THINGS TODAY

1. _____
2. _____
3. _____

I AM GOING TO ENJOY

1. _____
2. _____
3. _____

I NEED TO WORK ON

1. _____
2. _____

min - 1   2   3   4   5   6   7   8   9   10   11   12   13   14   15

#anote2self

DATE: / / TIME :

HOW CAN LACK OF SELF-LOVE AFFECT RELATIONSHIPS?

DEAR SELF,

MY INTENTIONS FOR TODAY ARE
1.
2.
3.

I AM THANKFUL FOR

I WILL ACCOMPLISH THESE THINGS TODAY
1.
2.
3.

I AM GOING TO ENJOY
1.
2.
3.

I NEED TO WORK ON
1.
2.

min - 1 2 3 4 5 6 7 8 9 10 11 12 13 14 15

#anote2self

DATE: / / TIME :

WHAT TYPE OF EXERCISES CAN HELP INDUCE MENTAL POSITIVITY?

DEAR SELF,

MY INTENTIONS FOR TODAY ARE
1.
2.
3.

I AM THANKFUL FOR

I WILL ACCOMPLISH THESE THINGS TODAY
1.
2.
3.

I AM GOING TO ENJOY
1.
2.
3.

I NEED TO WORK ON
1.
2.

min - 1 2 3 4 5 6 7 8 9 10 11 12 13 14 15

#anote2self

DATE: /   /   TIME   :

WHO ARE YOU WHEN NO ONE ELSE IS LOOKING?

DEAR SELF,

MY INTENTIONS FOR TODAY ARE

1.
2.
3.

I AM THANKFUL FOR

I WILL ACCOMPLISH THESE THINGS TODAY

1.
2.
3.

I AM GOING TO ENJOY

1.
2.
3.

I NEED TO WORK ON

1.
2.

min - 1   2   3   4   5   6   7   8   9   10   11   12   13   14   15

#anote2self

DATE: /   /   ◐   TIME   :

HOW DOES BEING IN TOUCH WITH TRANQUILITY INCREASE THE PROBABILITY
OF GOOD CHANGES?

DEAR SELF,

MY INTENTIONS FOR TODAY ARE
1.
2.
3.

I AM THANKFUL FOR

I WILL ACCOMPLISH THESE THINGS TODAY
1.
2.
3.

I AM GOING TO ENJOY
1.
2.
3.

I NEED TO WORK ON
1.
2.

min - 1   2   3   4   5   6   7   8   9   10   11   12   13   14   15

#anote2self

DATE: /   /   ◑   TIME   :

WHAT DO YOU NEED TO CREATE AN IDEAL MEDITATION SPACE?

_____
_____
_____
_____

DEAR SELF,

_____
_____
_____
_____
_____

MY INTENTIONS FOR TODAY ARE

1. _____
2. _____
3. _____

I AM THANKFUL FOR

_____

I WILL ACCOMPLISH THESE THINGS TODAY

1. _____
2. _____
3. _____

I AM GOING TO ENJOY

1. _____
2. _____
3. _____

I NEED TO WORK ON

1. _____
2. _____

min - 1   2   3   4   5   6   7   8   9   10   11   12   13   14   15

#anote2self

DATE: / / TIME :

HOW DOES MEDITATION STRENGTHEN THE CONNECTION OF THE MIND AND SPIRIT?

DEAR SELF,

MY INTENTIONS FOR TODAY ARE
1.
2.
3.

I AM THANKFUL FOR

I WILL ACCOMPLISH THESE THINGS TODAY
1.
2.
3.

I AM GOING TO ENJOY
1.
2.
3.

I NEED TO WORK ON
1.
2.

min - *1 2 3 4 5 6 7 8 9 10 11 12 13 14 15*
#anote2self

DATE: /   /   ◐   TIME   :

DEFINE LOVE.

_____
_____
_____
_____

DEAR SELF,

_____
_____
_____
_____

MY INTENTIONS FOR TODAY ARE

1. _____
2. _____
3. _____

I AM THANKFUL FOR

_____

I WILL ACCOMPLISH THESE THINGS TODAY

1. _____
2. _____
3. _____

I AM GOING TO ENJOY

1. _____
2. _____
3. _____

I NEED TO WORK ON

1. _____
2. _____

min - 1   2   3   4   5   6   7   8   9   10   11   12   13   14   15

#anote2self

DATE: / / ◖ TIME :

WHAT IS YOUR SUN NUMBER?

_____
_____
_____
_____

DEAR SELF,

_____
_____
_____
_____

MY INTENTIONS FOR TODAY ARE

1. _____
2. _____
3. _____

I AM THANKFUL FOR

_____

I WILL ACCOMPLISH THESE THINGS TODAY

1. _____
2. _____
3. _____

I AM GOING TO ENJOY

1. _____
2. _____
3. _____

I NEED TO WORK ON

1. _____
2. _____

min - 1 2 3 4 5 6 7 8 9 10 11 12 13 14 15

#anote2self

WHAT ARE EFFECTIVE TECHNIQUES FOR DECREASING TENSION AFTER A LONG DAY?

DEAR SELF,

MY INTENTIONS FOR TODAY ARE

1.
2.
3.

I AM THANKFUL FOR

I WILL ACCOMPLISH THESE THINGS TODAY

1.
2.
3.

I AM GOING TO ENJOY

1.
2.
3.

I NEED TO WORK ON

1.
2.

min - 1 2 3 4 5 6 7 8 9 10 11 12 13 14 15

#anote2self

DATE: / /   ◯   TIME :

WHAT SHOULD WE AVOID WHEN LEARNING HOW TO SELF-LOVE AND HEAL?

DEAR SELF,

MY INTENTIONS FOR TODAY ARE

1.
2.
3.

I AM THANKFUL FOR

I WILL ACCOMPLISH THESE THINGS TODAY

1.
2.
3.

I AM GOING TO ENJOY

1.
2.
3.

I NEED TO WORK ON

1.
2.

min - 1 2 3 4 5 6 7 8 9 10 11 12 13 14 15

#anote2self

DATE: /   /   TIME   :

WHAT ARE QUICK WAYS TO MAKE SURE YOU MAINTAIN YOUR COOL
IN STRESSFUL SITUATIONS?

DEAR SELF,

MY INTENTIONS FOR TODAY ARE

1.
2.
3.

I AM THANKFUL FOR

I WILL ACCOMPLISH THESE THINGS TODAY

1.
2.
3.

I AM GOING TO ENJOY

1.
2.
3.

I NEED TO WORK ON

1.
2.

min - 1   2   3   4   5   6   7   8   9   10   11   12   13   14   15

#anote2self

DATE: /   /   ◯   TIME   :

STATE YOUR SELF-LOVE CREED.

DEAR SELF,

MY INTENTIONS FOR TODAY ARE
1.
2.
3.

I AM THANKFUL FOR

I WILL ACCOMPLISH THESE THINGS TODAY
1.
2.
3.

I AM GOING TO ENJOY
1.
2.
3.

I NEED TO WORK ON
1.
2.

min - 1   2   3   4   5   6   7   8   9   10   11   12   13   14   15

#anote2self

DATE: /   /   ◑   TIME   :

HOW DO YOU CHANNEL NEGATIVE EXPERIENCES IN A POSITIVE WAY?

DEAR SELF,

MY INTENTIONS FOR TODAY ARE

1.
2.
3.

I AM THANKFUL FOR

I WILL ACCOMPLISH THESE THINGS TODAY

1.
2.
3.

I AM GOING TO ENJOY

1.
2.
3.

I NEED TO WORK ON

1.
2.

min - 1   2   3   4   5   6   7   8   9   10   11   12   13   14   15

#anote2self

DATE: / / TIME :

HOW COULD SPIRITUAL HEALING HELP THOSE WHO SELF-MEDICATE?

DEAR SELF,

MY INTENTIONS FOR TODAY ARE

1.
2.
3.

I AM THANKFUL FOR

I WILL ACCOMPLISH THESE THINGS TODAY

1.
2.
3.

I AM GOING TO ENJOY

1.
2.
3.

I NEED TO WORK ON

1.
2.

min - 1 2 3 4 5 6 7 8 9 10 11 12 13 14 15

#anote2self

DATE: /   /   ◑   TIME   :

DO YOU MEDITATE DAILY?

_____
_____
_____
_____

DEAR SELF,

_____
_____
_____
_____

MY INTENTIONS FOR TODAY ARE

1. _____
2. _____
3. _____

I AM THANKFUL FOR

_____

I WILL ACCOMPLISH THESE THINGS TODAY

1. _____
2. _____
3. _____

I AM GOING TO ENJOY

1. _____
2. _____
3. _____

I NEED TO WORK ON

1. _____
2. _____

min - 1   2   3   4   5   6   7   8   9   10   11   12   13   14   15

#anote2self

DATE: /   /   ◑   TIME   :

HOW LONG DID IT TAKE FOR MEDITATION TO MAKE A DIFFERENCE IN YOUR LIFE?
WHY?

_____
_____
_____

DEAR SELF,

_____
_____
_____
_____

MY INTENTIONS FOR TODAY ARE

1. _____
2. _____
3. _____

I AM THANKFUL FOR

_____

I WILL ACCOMPLISH THESE THINGS TODAY

1. _____
2. _____
3. _____

I AM GOING TO ENJOY

1. _____
2. _____
3. _____

I NEED TO WORK ON

1. _____
2. _____

min - 1   2   3   4   5   6   7   8   9   10   11   12   13   14   15

#anote2self

DATE: / / ◑ TIME :

WHEN DO YOU FIND TIME FOR SELF-CARE?

DEAR SELF,

MY INTENTIONS FOR TODAY ARE
1.
2.
3.

I AM THANKFUL FOR

I WILL ACCOMPLISH THESE THINGS TODAY
1.
2.
3.

I AM GOING TO ENJOY
1.
2.
3.

I NEED TO WORK ON
1.
2.

min - 1 2 3 4 5 6 7 8 9 10 11 12 13 14 15

#anote2self

DATE: /   /   ◑   TIME   :

WHAT DISTINCT PARTS MAKE UP YOUR MEDITATION SESSION?

DEAR SELF,

MY INTENTIONS FOR TODAY ARE
1.
2.
3.

I AM THANKFUL FOR

I WILL ACCOMPLISH THESE THINGS TODAY
1.
2.
3.

I AM GOING TO ENJOY
1.
2.
3.

I NEED TO WORK ON
1.
2.

min - 1   2   3   4   5   6   7   8   9   10   11   12   13   14   15

#anote2self

DATE: /   /   TIME   :

WHAT IS SOMETHING YOU MUST RELINQUISH TO ACHIEVE HAPPINESS?

DEAR SELF,

MY INTENTIONS FOR TODAY ARE

1.
2.
3.

I AM THANKFUL FOR

I WILL ACCOMPLISH THESE THINGS TODAY

1.
2.
3.

I AM GOING TO ENJOY

1.
2.
3.

I NEED TO WORK ON

1.
2.

min - *1   2   3   4   5   6   7   8   9   10   11   12   13   14   15*

#anote2self

DATE: /   /   ◑   TIME   :

CAN PEOPLE OF ALL AGES STUDY SELF-PRESERVATION? WHY OR WHY NOT?

_____
_____
_____
_____

DEAR SELF,

_____
_____
_____
_____

MY INTENTIONS FOR TODAY ARE

1. _____
2. _____
3. _____

I AM THANKFUL FOR

_____

I WILL ACCOMPLISH THESE THINGS TODAY

1. _____
2. _____
3. _____

I AM GOING TO ENJOY

1. _____
2. _____
3. _____

I NEED TO WORK ON

1. _____
2. _____

min - 1   2   3   4   5   6   7   8   9   10   11   12   13   14   15

#anote2self

DATE: / / TIME :

IF YOU GROW WISER INTERNALLY, HOW WILL IT POSITIVELY AFFECT THE EXTERNAL?

DEAR SELF,

MY INTENTIONS FOR TODAY ARE

1.
2.
3.

I AM THANKFUL FOR

I WILL ACCOMPLISH THESE THINGS TODAY

1.
2.
3.

I AM GOING TO ENJOY

1.
2.
3.

I NEED TO WORK ON

1.
2.

min - *1 2 3 4 5 6 7 8 9 10 11 12 13 14 15*

#anote2self

DATE: /   /   ◗   TIME   :

TO WHAT EXTENT DOES SELF-PRESERVATION DENOTE MAINTENANCE
OF PHYSICAL APPEARANCE?

DEAR SELF,

MY INTENTIONS FOR TODAY ARE

1.
2.
3.

I AM THANKFUL FOR

I WILL ACCOMPLISH THESE THINGS TODAY

1.
2.
3.

I AM GOING TO ENJOY

1.
2.
3.

I NEED TO WORK ON

1.
2.

min - 1   2   3   4   5   6   7   8   9   10   11   12   13   14   15

#anote2self

DATE: / / TIME :

WHAT ENVIRONMENT INSPIRES YOU?

DEAR SELF,

MY INTENTIONS FOR TODAY ARE
1.
2.
3.

I AM THANKFUL FOR

I WILL ACCOMPLISH THESE THINGS TODAY
1.
2.
3.

I AM GOING TO ENJOY
1.
2.
3.

I NEED TO WORK ON
1.
2.

min - 1 2 3 4 5 6 7 8 9 10 11 12 13 14 15
#anote2self

DATE: /   /   ●   TIME   :

HOW DOES ART HELP YOU HEAL?

_____
_____
_____
_____

DEAR SELF,

_____
_____
_____
_____

MY INTENTIONS FOR TODAY ARE

1. _____
2. _____
3. _____

I AM THANKFUL FOR

_____

I WILL ACCOMPLISH THESE THINGS TODAY

1. _____
2. _____
3. _____

I AM GOING TO ENJOY

1. _____
2. _____
3. _____

I NEED TO WORK ON

1. _____
2. _____

min - 1   2   3   4   5   6   7   8   9   10   11   12   13   14   15

#anote2self

You made it to the end of your journal!

You should be proud that you were able to spend such a good amount of time on (and with) yourself. Thank you for being open and honest through your evolution and meditation process. Your entries show not only growth but also self-discovery. The #ANote2Self meditation journal was created to tailor your specific spiritual needs. Whatever your desires were for journaling on these pages, you brought to fruition by simply writing them into existence. My hope is that you felt a sense of connection to yourself that you might have lost sight of or even forgotten. Keep investing in your higher self and wellbeing! You have taken the initial step by completing your #ANote2Self journal.

With love + light,
Alex Elle

APPENDIX

JANUARY

Named after the Roman god Janus—a deity of doorways and passages—January is a month of new beginnings, transitions, and emergence. Periods of hibernation must come to an end. This may include letting go of a bad relationship, the search for a new job, or a change in perspective. The full moon in January has been referred to as the Wolf Moon because of its association with hungry, howling wolves who have managed to get through a rough winter and who are ready to hunt. Accordingly, looking to your pack, taming your animal instincts, and connecting with the season are all encouraged. While the whole year is rich with potential for personal growth, January is an especially great month to shed old unneeded skins, lean on those around you, and move forward with respectability.

FEBRUARY

The month's impact on the day-to-day phases of the moon can sometimes be difficult to follow, but insight abounds for those with the patience and curiosity to familiarize themselves with the details. February is a month for continuing transitional behavior, and for love, fertility and purification. With spring on the way, ideas of spiritual cleansing, renewal, and change should be on your mind. The word February is derived from a Latin word meaning, "to purify." So carry on what you started in January, or pick back up something—a life focus—you may have released in the past year. The full moons of February have been referred to as the Snow Moons in honor of the sometimes harsh conditions that may occur during this time of the year, but this month asks you to remember that whatever "winter" you may have been going through is ready and willing to depart whenever you wish.

MARCH

The moons of March have been referred to as the Crow Moon, the Magpie Moon, and the Worm Moon by various cultures because spring draws near in March and affects the earth and its inhabitants. The birds of the sky emerge singing farewells to the winter and the worms beneath reveal themselves in preparation for the oncoming season. The month is named after the Roman god of war Mars who, before becoming known for his strength, was associated with agriculture, cycles, and growth — reminding us that the time for melting away the old baggage of winter is upon us. Ultimately, March brings with it focus, momentum, triumph, and warm energy. Revitalize yourself, your beliefs, and your relationships this month. Each day is emboldened by this month's power.

APRIL

The full moon of this month has the been referred to as the Growing Moon because the Earth is changing, spring is in full swing, and the plants are in bloom. Many believe that April was named after the Latin word aperire, meaning"to open", that alludes to the opening of the flowers and the many opportunities for personal growth. April is strongly tied to ideas of birth, rebirth, and development. So think about what needs gardening in your life because April is ripe with renewal.

MAY

The full moon of May is deftly referred to as the Flower Moon. Like the name suggests, the lunar energy of this month brings with it an increasing sense of growth. Continue ventures from last month or simply use the momentum of May to start something new. Been putting something off? Meaning to get around to something? Well, get on it! Because whatever the case, cherishing loved ones, respecting yourself, and seeking to improve your situation are all warmly smiled upon in May.

JUNE

June was named after Juno—a powerful Roman goddess of marriage and family. Accordingly, June is most associated with ideas of fidelity, commitment, and loyalty. Reflect on what needs your commitment; it may even be that you simply need to commit to yourself. In June, crops are ripening and summer blankets the world. The sun shines for longer periods of time in the day, offering more hours for project completion. The full moon in June has commonly been referred to as the Strawberry Moon because this was the point when strawberries were at their ripest, just as your opportunities are ripe in the month of June—they are charged with strong solar energy and cheerful vibrations.

JULY

Traditionally, this time of year—specifically, the end of July—has been honored as a midway point between the summer solstice (the first day of summer) and the autumnal equinox (the first day of spring). July also contains the beginning of the harvest season and reminds us to start planting seeds for the future and gardening the relationships of our lives. Ultimately, July is an ideal time for making plans, being grateful, and spending time with loves ones. Consider what you'd like to work on and challenge yourself.

AUGUST

Much of the sentiment of July pours into August, making this month the continuation of solar influences, the celebration of light, and the beginning of the harvest. Every day, with every decision, we are planting seeds to be sown. When we invest our time and energy in someone or something and hope that our efforts will be fruitful, we are planting seeds in hopes of a better future. August vibrations urge ambition, hope, and action. The full moon in August has a few names, each of which emphasize fire—the Red Moon in honor of the subtle hues of crimson sometimes seen within it—and gain—the Sturgeon Moon since fishing is viewed as a promising endeavor in August. So cast your net, hold your head high, and burn with the power and excitement of August inside of you.

SEPTEMBER

Naturally, the full moon of this month has been called the Harvest Moon. September is all about winding down, transformation, acceptance, and giving thanks. Fall is quietly moving in and, with it, comes all the symbolism of change. The days have equal amounts of light and dark, reminding us to seek balance and moderation and to accept the bad with the good. Besides, how can we appreciate the good without an understanding of the bad? September is for counting blessings, and represents the slowing of the harvest season. Be sure to appreciate all that you have.

OCTOBER

Historically, at this point, the crops had been cleared, harvested, and stored in preparation of the oncoming winter, which allowed hunters to detect their prey more efficiently. This lends October's full moon the name of the Hunters' Moon. It is no coincidence that October is for seeing. Legend has it that the veil between this world and whatever lies beyond is at its thinnest and most gossamer during the month of October. Our senses hold the power to become alive with intuition, knowing, and an awareness. This a powerful period for deep self-discovery, honoring the dead, and appreciating the extraordinary.

NOVEMBER

Still fall, November trudges forth with remnants of October energy clinging to its coattails. With fall still in full swing, we are reminded to let go of what no longer serves us and to embrace change. The loss of a job or a loved one is not only an ending, but a new, different, and challenging beginning. Just as the lunar cycles are constantly changing, so too are you. Though sometimes frightening, change is truly a blessing as it holds the potential for new growth. On a historical and contemporary level, November is about putting time aside to remember and pay homage to people who have passed. Metaphorically, you may even mourn and celebrate the death of an old version of yourself. November prays for peace and whispers of wisdom for those who offer an ear. Native Americans called the November moon the Beaver Moon because it was a very important time for gathering furs for the winter. Similarly, don't damn your vulnerabilities; instead, take time to self-preserve and tend to your needs.

DECEMBER

December concerns itself with the celebration of light. Before long, both spring and the sunshine will return; in the meantime, December reminds us of our need for warmth. So light a fire in the hearth, burn a candle at your bedside or have a cozy bonfire with friends. Take heed and recall that all of the coldness and pitfalls represented by winter are only temporary. Remember that they help you to grow. December full moons have been called the Cold Moons or the Long Night Moons because of the chilly atmosphere of the earth at this time and the prolonged periods of nightfall. Look for the light in your life. Know that it never goes away even if it seems far at a times. You have likely learned that not everything is always as it seems, and that, oftentimes, there is a subtle tugging of strings, energies, and destinies in many different directions. Celebrate your life and all the promise it brings.

NEW MOON

Day 1

The seeming absence of the moon in the sky reminds its children that the possibilities are endless during this time. As the moon is reborn anew, so are you. This is not a time to dwell on the past, rather, it is a time for rejoicing in new beginnings. Intimately introduce yourself to all of the opportunities in your life, and seek knowledge about the direction in which you wish to travel next. Ask yourself where you can best invest your energy because the time is nigh for pursuits of all shapes and sizes.

WAXING CRESCENT

Day 2

1 — Efforts to strengthen yourself during a waxing crescent moon are emboldened by the energies of this lunar phase. Pour yourself into the good things in your life and taste the Universe's blessings on your tongue. Remember that your past experiences were necessary ingredients, each playing a part in bringing you to where you are now. Look back on what you have gone through and congratulate yourself.

Day 3

2 — Still hardly visible, this Cheshire Cat smile of a moon whispers to those who listen that luck is on their side. During the new moon, you looked at all of the possibilities at your fingertips, and now it's a time to narrow down your options. Is it love that you seek, or seek to improve? Wealth, friendship, health, courage, or self-esteem? Determine what it is you need most. The moon is growing now; allow your goals to blossom with it.

Day 4

3 — Consider and envision. Ask yourself, "If my wishes were to come true, what would that look like in my life? What do I need to do?" Start unfolding a plan and laying groundwork. Look at all of the different angles. Focus on the practical steps required to move you smoothly through this journey, and do so knowing that the momentum of this moon is behind you. Transformation need not be complicated. It can be as simple as one tiny decision you make differently each day.

Day 5

4 — This day offers many opportunities to breathe life into your plans. There is no room for insecurity, procrastination, or second-guessing. There will be a time for personal reflection later, after the appearance of the full moon. For now, this moon speaks of gain, increase, and growth. It encourages you to make your move and to do so passionately. Your destiny is your own story to write.

Day 6

5 — It is true what they say: For every action, there is an equal and opposite reaction. If you have been tuning into the energy of the recent moons, you may have noticed how the people and events around you are shifting too. This is evidence of your own personal power, the Universe alive inside of you, and the channeled energy of the moon. Some people—perhaps even yourself—are resistant to change, but do not allow this to derail you from your sacred purpose. Move forward with grace, strength, and tact.

WAXING CRESCENT CONTINUATION

Day 7

6 — Aligning yourself with lunar energies comes with a newfound awareness of the subtle shifts in day-to-day energy. If this sounds familiar, just keep doing what you are doing, and your intuition will only expand. If this is not something you feel yet, give it some time. Everyone's voyage proceeds at a different pace, and it is those glorious differences that make us each so unique. Today, the moon asks you to look around to see if there is someone in your life who could benefit from something you could teach, or if there's someone in your life whose wisdom could benefit you. Do not be afraid to reach out.

FIRST QUARTER MOON

Day 8

Do you feel it now—the momentous first quarter moon shocking alive your sense of knowing and intuition? Trust your instincts today because they are unlikely to let you down. This is an excellent time for decision-making, but remember to do things with a level head. There is no need for extremes. Even the appearance of the first quarter moon—with one half of darkness and the other half of light—encourages balance. So look at things from all sides, stay in control of your emotions, and feel free to make big decisions.

WAXING GIBBOUS

Day 9

1 — Take a moment, take a deep breath. Yesterday's moon represented a big step in your journey, and today is about relaxation. If you've been working towards a goal, do something to celebrate the time and thought you have invested in it. Always remember that you deserve and are worthy of celebration. Today's moon is about honoring yourself.

Day 10

2 — Perhaps you have noticed how the moon is growing in the sky. There is a sense of momentum as the full moon draws near. You may wish to use this opportunity to start a project or do something you have been meaning to do. Figure out if there is any unfinished business in your life and determine what has been holding you back. Move forward with love, strength, and endurance because the power of the moon is expanding, and with it, so are your horizons.

Day 11

3 — If you truly want something, give yourself permission to have it. Your heart is a cathedral of the divine and the beautiful. There simply isn't room for worry or hesitation. Promise yourself greatness, and know that you have the power to create and obtain it. This evening's moon carries with it an aura of courage and triumph, so don't be afraid to use it.

WAXING GIBBOUS CONTINUATION

Day 12

4 — Surrounding yourself with things that you love is a powerful way of improving your quality of life. What is it that fulfills you? Set aside a couple of minutes to do what makes you happy. Maybe it's taking the time to catch up with an old friend, to take a nap, to read, to eat something delicious, or to get some fresh air. If you lack the time or resources to engage in such an activity, you can either devote a portion of your day to appreciating it or make future plans to partake.

Day 13

5 — Your heavenly connection with this nearly full moon cries of luck, wealth, and health. The power of the moon is nearly at its peak, and so is your opportunity to take advantage of it. Fullness, promise, and attainment belong to those who sync themselves with this moon. Reaching out for what you want is highly recommended, and if you are behind in anything, now is a great time for catching up. If there isn't anything particularly lacking in your life, then consider what you can do to make the world a better place. The waxing gibbous offers power.

Day 14

6 — You may experience a temporary pause in your endeavors, or something may be preoccupying your thoughts. Tonight's moon can have that effect on people. Do not interpret this as a bad omen, but rather, as a moment of reprieve before the moon reaches its peak. This day calls for patience, project completion, tying off of loose ends, and faith in the Universe. Continue your regeneration and collect your thoughts.

FULL MOON

Day 15

The moon presents you with opportunity, power, and clarity. It is not uncommon for those beneath this moon to feel a stirring in their bones or a sense of restlessness. Potential is at its height for all actions, but also for all reactions. While it is easy to draw in this moon's energy, people are also susceptible to overreactions. So live fully, but take care to monitor your internal emotional states. Instead of spending time on people or actions that have the potential to aggravate, chose instead to be with those who lighten your spirit and engage in activities that enhance your happiness. This is the single most powerful day in the entire lunar cycle as it represents a great transition in your journey, so take advantage of the infinite possibilities and trust in yourself.

WANING GIBBOUS

Day 16

1 — The bolstering attitude of the recent full moon still lingers, but the period for slowing down is gently descending upon you. Little by little, the moon will become smaller, symbolizing the processes of letting go, release, and forgiveness. Things are now shifting into a more introspective tone, which makes this period ideal for personal growth. Take a much needed break, take a bath, or eat something fresh from the Earth. Lie beneath a newly laundered blanket or appreciate the graceful glory of nature. Always remind yourself that you deserve and are worthy of profound self-care.

Day 17

2 — Your life is made up of millions of tiny blessings woven into the fabric of every passing moment. The breath in your lungs, the melody of a loved one's laughter, and a brand new day are all tiny gifts, each tailored and offered specifically to you. Lessening in size by the day, the moon symbolizes surrender. So give yourself over to the plethora of goodness in your precious life, and appreciate the divinity that every moment hungrily waits for you to notice.

Day 18

3 — While yesterday was a day of personal awareness, today is a day of external gratefulness. Thank the things that make your life better. Is it music, art, a person, a pet, or your job? Make today about expressing your gratitude. Use the atmosphere of this waning gibbous to pull closer the things you appreciate most by paying homage to the contributions they make in your life.

Day 19

4 — Everyone has a vice, however small or secret. People all do things they truly shouldn't. Today is for thinking about what outside thing is pointless in your life. Have you been hiding from a truth, self-medicating, or seeking escape? Reflect on your own actions, and create a mental list of positive activities or actions that can replace them. Keep these bad habits and alternative courses of action in your mind as you move through the day.

Day 20

5 — It can be very difficult to let go of things that are no longer good for you in your life. Take small steps to let go of the actions, thoughts, or people who bring down your existence. Your happiness can only be as great as the lack of unhappiness in your life. Thus, it is important that you begin to remove the elements that fail to make you happy.

Day 21

6 — Remember that personal growth and spiritual evolution is an ongoing process. While it would be wonderful if change could happen overnight, this is seldom the case. Be patient with your journey, knowing that the rate at which you are blooming is the right rate for you. Moving forward requires a commitment to self-evaluation, behavioral changes, and making promises to yourself. Use this time to continue your personal discovery. The eve before the last quarter moon offers help to those who are willing to shed their old skin.

LAST QUARTER MOON

Day 22

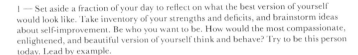

The last quarter moon introduces another important step in your travels. The total lunar cycle is coming to a close, which may translate into a minor mental crisis since the new moon is only days away. The moon itself is half lit; your own life may mirror this. You may find yourself half in and half out of something, but not entirely sure of how to proceed. Tension may be higher than usual, or something may be uniquely challenging today. Do your best to tread lightly. Don't forget that, inside of you, you have everything you need to work through any obstacles.

WANING CRESCENT

Day 23

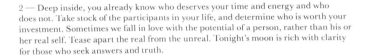

1 — Set aside a fraction of your day to reflect on what the best version of yourself would look like. Take inventory of your strengths and deficits, and brainstorm ideas about self-improvement. Be who you want to be. How would the most compassionate, enlightened, and beautiful version of yourself think and behave? Try to be this person today. Lead by example.

Day 24

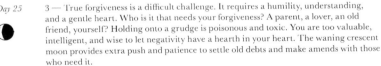

2 — Deep inside, you already know who deserves your time and energy and who does not. Take stock of the participants in your life, and determine who is worth your investment. Sometimes we fall in love with the potential of a person, rather than his or her real self. Tease apart the real from the unreal. Tonight's moon is rich with clarity for those who seek answers and truth.

Day 25

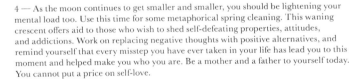

3 — True forgiveness is a difficult challenge. It requires a humility, understanding, and a gentle heart. Who is it that needs your forgiveness? A parent, a lover, an old friend, yourself? Holding onto a grudge is poisonous and toxic. You are too valuable, intelligent, and wise to let negativity have a hearth in your heart. The waning crescent moon provides extra push and patience to settle old debts and make amends with those who need it.

Day 26

4 — As the moon continues to get smaller and smaller, you should be lightening your mental load too. Use this time for some metaphorical spring cleaning. This waning crescent offers aid to those who wish to shed self-defeating properties, attitudes, and addictions. Work on replacing negative thoughts with positive alternatives, and remind yourself that every misstep you have ever taken in your life has lead you to this moment and helped make you who you are. Be a mother and a father to yourself today. You cannot put a price on self-love.

WANING CRESCENT CONTINUATION

Day 27

5 —You might have noticed how much of the waxing moons revolve around ideas of development, obtainment, and the attraction of positive energy, while much of the waning moons ask you to focus on inward expansion, freedom from negativity, and reflection. With the new moon just around the corner, the waning crescent asks you to embark on the difficult task of making amends with those who you have wronged— taking responsibility for your thoughts and deeds, and asking for forgiveness where necessary. This day is for healing.

Day 28

6 —Hibernation and laying low are optimal now. Invest inward. This does not mean that you must be a hermit—but hold your tongue, listen more (and listen closely), and be slow to act. Tomorrow brings the final step in this lunar cycle, making today the last day for the banishment of bad vibes, negative outlooks, or people who prove themselves to be less than what your holy existence deserves. The appearance of the moon is nearly invisible in the sky now, and so too should be any baggage you have been carrying. Grant yourself the precious freedom, confidence, and bravery to do what you must.

#ANOTE2SELF

—

Meditation Journal
by
Alex Elle

INSTAGRAM: @ALEX_ELLE

INSTAGRAM: @ANOTE2SELFJOURNAL

Made in the USA
Columbia, SC
08 October 2018